IMAGES
of America

FORT MONMOUTH

THE JOHNSTON GATE. Originally dedicated around 1961 and rededicated on April 18, 1986, the Johnston Gate memorializes Col. Gordon Johnston. Johnston received the Congressional Medal of Honor for gallantry in battle during the Philippine Insurrection. The brick arches were constructed in 1985 and 1986 as part of the post beautification plan. Col. William. A. Mackinnon, Headquarters and Installation Support Activity, and James Ott, Directorate of Engineering and Housing, directed the project. Architectural and site designs were completed by Wallace and Watson Associates of Bethlehem, Pennsylvania. (Courtesy of the U.S. Army CECOM Life Cycle Management Command Historical Archives.)

On the cover: **WIRE CLASS, C. 1920.** Soldiers participate in a wire class, climbing telegraph poles. Field wire techniques became a formal part of the installation repair course at the Signal Corps School, where men regularly learned how to construct and climb poles. (Courtesy of the U.S. Army CECOM Life Cycle Management Command Historical Archives.)

IMAGES
of America

FORT MONMOUTH

Wendy A. Rejan

ARCADIA
PUBLISHING

Published by Arcadia Publishing
Charleston SC, Chicago IL, Portsmouth NH, San Francisco CA

Printed in the United States of America

Library of Congress Control Number: 2009923440

For all general information contact Arcadia Publishing at:
Telephone 843-853-2070
Fax 843-853-0044
E-mail sales@arcadiapublishing.com
For customer service and orders:
Toll-Free 1-888-313-2665

Visit us on the Internet at www.arcadiapublishing.com

*This book is dedicated to all the civilian, military, and contractor
personnel who have worked or lived at Fort Monmouth.*

CONTENTS

ACKNOWLEDGMENTS

Thanks first and foremost must go to Melissa Ziobro, Floyd Hertweck, and Chrissie Reilly, staff historians, for their assistance with research, editing captions, and locating and scanning photographs. To Michael Brady, my boss, thank you for always being supportive of the history program and providing thoughtful input and suggestions. Thank you to the Fort Monmouth photographers from Chenega Technology Services Corporation and, previously, the Signal Corps. Thank you to all those military, civilian, and contractor personnel who have donated photographs to the history office archives over the years. Thanks also to our personnel who, while deployed to Southwest Asia, took photographs to ensure that history was preserved. Thanks to the previous historians and archivists who cared for the documents and photographs that went into making this book. And finally, thanks to Maj. Gen. Dennis L. Via, an avid supporter of celebrating and preserving Fort Monmouth's history. All images, unless otherwise noted, are courtesy of the U.S. Army CECOM Life Cycle Management Command Historical Archives.

INTRODUCTION

Established in June 1917 during World War I, Fort Monmouth has been the epicenter for the U.S. Army's communications and electronics mission for close to a century. From its humble beginnings as a signal training camp at Little Silver, the post evolved into the home of the Signal Corps and, today, home of the U.S. Army CECOM Life Cycle Management Command. For generations, dedicated military and civilian scientists, engineers, logisticians, program managers, and support staff have toiled around the clock to ensure the nation's servicemen and servicewomen were equipped with the very best communications and electronics (C-E) equipment possible. The pursuit of this noble endeavor garnered Fort Monmouth the affectionate label the "army's house of magic."

All manner of strange images awaited a visitor touring the main post and its local satellite stations many years ago, including pigeons flying overhead; giant turntables slowing rotating various vehicles; soldiers chasing balloons, scaling telephone poles, or testing walkie-talkies; combat photographers in training; unattended vehicles operating of their own accord; giant radars and antennas; strange igloo-shaped huts; and electronic equipment acclimating to the particular conditions of arctic and tropical chambers. All manner of fantastic experiments occurred within the walls of laboratories where dangerous isotopes and lethal doses of voltage abounded.

Continuing today in various laboratories, these lifesaving developments include three-dimensional virtual prototyping, battery testing, interactive speech technology, laser and counter infrared technologies, radar development, acoustic mine detection, human test and perception, humanitarian demining, unmanned aerial vehicles, antenna modeling and simulation, cryptographic modernization, satellite and radio communications, and subterranean communications, as well as facilities for sense through the wall technologies, prototype fabrication, a flight activity to test C-E payloads, and an anechoic chamber, to name just a few. The personnel working in these facilities have garnered many high awards in recent years, and several inventions and systems are named as top 10 U.S. Army inventions. Many of these inventions are now being used by troops in Afghanistan and Iraq.

The installation has gone by several names since its establishment, the first of which was Camp Little Silver in June 1917; it was referred to colloquially by many of the soldiers as Camp Monmouth. In September 1917, it achieved semipermanent status and was renamed Camp Alfred Vail, which it went by until 1925 when it was renamed Fort Monmouth. Just as the name of the installation has changed, so have the organizations located on Fort Monmouth gone by many names over the years. These include the Signal Corps Laboratories, Signal School, Signal Corps Center, Electronics Command (ECOM), Communications, Research and Development Command (CORADCOM), Communications-Electronics Readiness Command (CERCOM), Communications-Electronics Command (CECOM), Program Executive Offices (PEO), and countless resident activities that have come and gone. Despite the numerous reorganizations and name changes, the primary mission of supporting the life-cycle management of C-E equipment has remained constant.

Fort Monmouth's long signal-related history is evident in the turn of every street and the name of every building. Numerous monuments grace tree-lined avenues and pay homage to both heroes and scientists. The names Myer, Armstrong, Squier, and Blair reflect an illustrious history of innovation and service to country. This heritage was not isolated to the post—it also touched the surrounding communities. As Fort Monmouth underwent its most significant expansion during World War II, leased facilities included the famed Asbury Park Convention Center and land as far south as the Toms River. Today remnants of this relationship can be found all over Monmouth and Ocean Counties and include the old Marconi site in Wall Township.

This small U.S. Army installation near the New Jersey seashore has produced equipment and systems that have changed and shaped the course of history. The decision to use FM (frequency modulation) radio and the invention of radar here helped to win World War II. The fort ushered in the space age with cutting-edge technology that bounced signals off the moon and produced the world's first communications satellite. Revolutionary items fielded during the Vietnam era included lighter, more portable radios and night vision devices. Today the systems the fort supports help to keep troops safe in Southwest Asia by locating hostile firing positions, increasing situational awareness, and intercepting improvised explosive devices.

Not only did Fort Monmouth lead the way with cutting-edge C-E systems, it also paved the way socially by employing women and African Americans in highly technical fields well ahead of the outside world. The first contingent of the Women's Army Auxiliary Corps arrived at the post in 1943. The highly technical nature of the work performed at the fort led many women into nontraditional careers requiring advanced knowledge in engineering. The Signal Corps at Fort Monmouth also offered unique opportunities for African Americans in the 1940s and 1950s, resulting in the label of the post as the "black brain center" of the United States. These pioneers blazed a trail for successive achievements by women and African Americans, including the first African American woman to achieve the GS-14 grade and the first African American general in the history of the Signal Corps. When asked how he would like Fort Monmouth to be remembered, former deputy to the commanding general Victor Ferlise said, "As a place where twenty years before the civil rights movement, African Americans could do great things."

Today scientists and engineers in the Communications-Electronics Research, Development, and Engineering Center (CERDEC) work to develop and integrate command, control, communications, computers, intelligence, surveillance, and reconnaissance (C4ISR) systems. Contracting experts negotiate with industry partners to award contracts for manufacturing these systems. Program managers work to acquire and field them. Behind the scenes, logisticians ensure that these products get to the right people at the right place at the right time. Logistics experts teach soldiers how to use them and also deploy alongside the units they support. And software engineers and personnel at the command's depot work around the clock to maintain and repair that equipment.

Fort Monmouth has come to symbolize much more than just a paycheck for its workers. For many people who started out at the fort in their first job after college or who came here on their first big promotion, this installation and mission have come to symbolize their devotion to meaningful work—work that impacts the lives of soldiers. It is also a place that has provided an extended network of friends and family—bonds that have been built up over decades. For many employees, Fort Monmouth is irrevocably caught up with their childhood too—with days spent at the bowling alley or miniature golf course and nights at the infamous teen club.

The impact of Fort Monmouth's personnel and cutting-edge technology is incalculable; its legacy is in the countless lives that have been saved from World War I to current operations in Southwest Asia. In the words of Maj. Gen. Dennis L. Via, "If you were to remove the historic technological contributions to the modern world made by Fort Monmouth, this would be a much less advanced and much less enlightened world."

One

PRE-ARMY DAYS TO CAMP ALFRED VAIL

RACETRACK TICKET BOOTH. As America prepared to enter World War I, the U.S. Army recognized that it would need additional sites to train Signal Corps troops. Maj. Gen. Charles H. Corlett (Ret.) located this land, once known as the Monmouth Park Race Track, in May 1917. Remnants of the track lay everywhere and included this former ticket booth. The first camp was known as Camp Little Silver, based on its proximity to the town of Little Silver.

MONMOUTH PARK HOTEL, C. 1890. The racetrack's luxury hotel fronted Parker Creek. Many of the celebrities and dignitaries of the day graced the grounds, including actress Lily Langtry, opera singer Lillian Russell, tobacco millionaire Pierre Lorilard, and English poet Alfred Lord Tennyson. The hotel had 153 rooms and included an electric elevator, a smoking room, billiard rooms, glass chandeliers, silk tapestries, baroque staircases, and oriental rugs.

RACETRACK GRANDSTAND IN RUINS. The track closed in 1893 when the New Jersey legislature outlawed gambling. The prime stake of the season, the Jersey Derby, moved to Louisville, Kentucky. Deserted, the grandstand, track, and hotel fell into ruin. A storm decimated the grandstand in 1899, and the hotel burned to the ground in 1915. Just two years later, the U.S. Army leased 468 acres of the site with an option to buy.

ADVANCE PARTY, 1917. The first 32 Signal Corps soldiers arrived at Fort Monmouth on June 3, 1917, in two Ford Model T trucks. First Lt. Adolph J. Dekker led the advance party and brought tents, tools, and other equipment from Bedloe's Island, New York, to prepare the site. By June 14, soldiers cleared several acres and established a cantonment, quartermaster facility, and camp hospital under canvas.

CAMP LITTLE SILVER, JUNE 1917. This encampment was located immediately inside the east gate. At the top of the photograph, the former racetrack ticket booth is visible. The soldiers set up camp and awaited the arrival of lumber to build barracks. Cpl. Carl L. Whitehurst was among the first men to arrive at Camp Little Silver. He later recalled that the site appeared to be a "jungle of weeds, poison ivy, briars, and underbrush."

FIRST TROOPS AT CAMP LITTLE SILVER, 1917. The men survived their first winter, and Signal Corps training embarked amid the fire-gutted ruins of the racetrack and Charles Prothero's potato farm. By the end of 1918, this was called the best-equipped Signal Corps camp ever established. Just 19 months after its acquisition by the military, 129 semipermanent structures stood. Housing could accommodate 2,975 soldiers and 188 officers.

SOLDIERS LINE UP FOR INOCULATIONS. Illness was common at the early camp, as the troops spent much of their time clearing the undergrowth. In the first month of the camp's existence, 19 soldiers were hospitalized for poison ivy exposure. That number had skyrocketed to 129 by July. The 122nd Aero Squadron was quarantined when it arrived in March 1918 due to several cases of measles.

HOSPITAL CORPS, CAMP LITTLE SILVER. Instruction for the first trainees in July 1917 included camp sanitation, personal hygiene, and first aid. Establishing urinals and latrines was one of the first important jobs at a new camp. Unsanitary conditions and the contamination of groundwater posed a serious health threat. Human and horse refuse had to be carefully disposed of. Refuse and animal carcasses were often burned or buried.

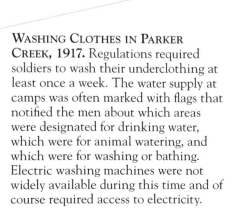

WASHING CLOTHES IN PARKER CREEK, 1917. Regulations required soldiers to wash their underclothing at least once a week. The water supply at camps was often marked with flags that notified the men about which areas were designated for drinking water, which were for animal watering, and which were for washing or bathing. Electric washing machines were not widely available during this time and of course required access to electricity.

HANGARS TWO AND THREE AND THE REPAIR SHOP. The particular demands of aerial warfare during World War I led the U.S. Army to devote part of the mission at Camp Alfred Vail to researching ground-to-air radios. Heddon Construction Company built two airfields and four hangars east of Oceanport Avenue. Over 90 test flights were being made per week in 1918, leading local residents to mistakenly believe the camp was an airfield.

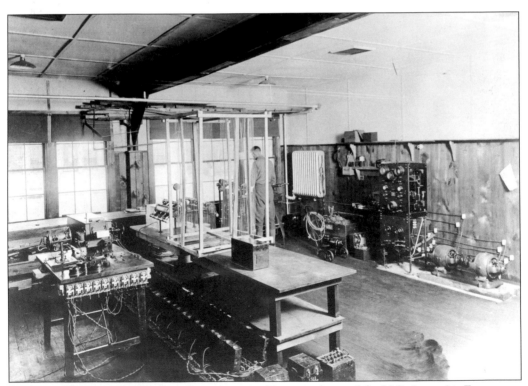

AIRPLANE DIRECTION-FINDING LABORATORY. Two squadrons of the U.S. Army Air Force were assigned to Camp Alfred Vail in 1918. The 504th Aero Squadron arrived in February 1918, consisting of one officer and 100 enlisted men. The first planes, along with the 122nd Aero Squadron, arrived in March 1918. This squadron consisted of 12 officers and 157 enlisted men. The camp produced the first ground-to-air radios put into military production.

SOLDIER AND AIRCRAFT. A total of 20 aircraft constituted the flying activity at Camp Alfred Vail. These included two DeHaviland 4s, nine Curtiss JN4-Hs, six Curtiss 4-6Hos, and three Curtiss JN-4Ds. Following the signing of the armistice in November 1918, the aviation section was moved from the camp. In its short time, it had, however, made enormous headway in adapting radio to aircraft for World War I.

MOCKER, WORLD WAR I HERO HOMING PIGEON. On September 12, 1918, heavy enemy artillery fire was blocking the American advance into the Alsace-Lorraine sector of France. With an eye destroyed by a shell fragment and his head a mass of clotted blood, Mocker homed in record time from the vicinity of Beaumont with a message giving the exact location of specific enemy heavy artillery batteries. Mocker died at Fort Monmouth in June 1937.

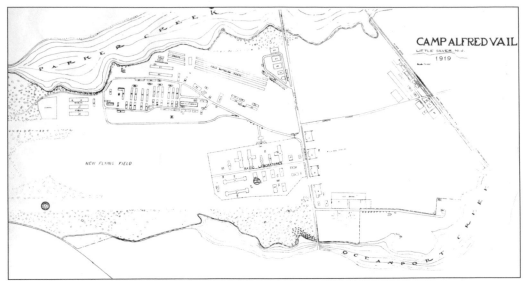

MAP OF CAMP ALFRED VAIL, 1919. The camp achieved semipermanent status and was renamed Camp Alfred Vail in September 1917, just three months after its establishment. Vail, an associate of telegraph inventor Samuel F. B. Morse, was credited with helping him develop commercial telegraphy. The flying field is marked on this map, as are the radio laboratories, the New York-to-Long Branch rail line, Parker Creek, field battalion tents, stables, and Oceanport Creek.

AERIAL, CAMP ALFRED VAIL, 1923. This photograph shows the outline of one of the former running tracks of the Monmouth Park Race Track. The original track, built in 1870, was located in the vicinity of Patterson Army Health Clinic. A new larger park, designed by D. Withers, opened in 1890. It covered 640 acres of the land that became Fort Monmouth. The racetrack encompassed almost all of what is today the main post.

RADIO LABORATORIES, JANUARY 1919. Construction for the radio laboratories began in December 1917, resulting in 43 semipermanent laboratory buildings. Research initially centered on vacuum tubes, circuits of existing equipment, testing equipment submitted by manufacturers, and the application of new inventions. A staff of 48 officers, 45 enlisted men, and 12 civilians accomplished this work.

CAMP HEADQUARTERS. Construction of the old wooden camp began in the summer of 1917. Laborers worked overtime to complete a headquarters building, officers' quarters, barracks, transportation sheds, shops, and a warehouse near the railroad siding.

HOSPITAL, CAMP ALFRED VAIL. This hospital was equipped to handle 40 patients. The camp was hit particularly hard by the influenza outbreak that struck the nation in September 1918. As outbreaks occurred, units were quarantined until eventually the entire camp was isolated. By the time the quarantine ended in November, 11 deaths had occurred, and the hospital treated a total of 267 cases.

A Favorite indoor Sport
At Camp Vail

POSTCARD, CAMP ALFRED VAIL. This postcard was published by the Young Men's Christian Association at Camp Alfred Vail. Other early postcards included pictures of soldiers drilling at the camp and riding horses. Postcards were a convenient way to keep in touch with loved ones back home and to show them what the camp looked like.

COMPANY C, 10TH FIELD SIGNAL BATTALION, 1917. Pictured from left to right are Smith, Parks, Dawson, Hoke, and Arnold. The 10th Signal Corps battalion was organized at Camp Alfred Vail on July 10, 1917. The battalion was assigned to the 7th Division, U.S. Army (regular). It departed the installation on August 17, 1918, saw frontline action in France, and had its colors decorated by Gen. John J. Pershing on May 9, 1919.

RESERVE OFFICERS' TRAINING CORPS STUDENTS. The Morrill Act established the Reserve Officers' Training Corps (ROTC) in 1862. Training of ROTC personnel, which began here in June 1920, developed into a major function of the Signal School. These students arrived at Camp Alfred Vail around 1921. Signal ROTC courses presented in prominent universities throughout the United States trained radio operators and telegraphers. During World War II, nearly 50 percent of officer candidate school enrollees at Fort Monmouth were ROTC students.

SOLDIERS DELOUSING UNIFORMS, 1918. Camp hygiene was a recurring problem in its initial years before the advent of running water and modern plumbing. Lice infestation presented a significant issue, and maintaining clean clothing was known to be essential to preventing it.

ENLISTED SPECIALISTS. These specialists are conducting laboratory work in telegraphy at the Signal Corps School, Camp Alfred Vail. The initial Signal Corps School curriculum included cryptography, heliograph, semaphore, wigwag, motor vehicle operation, physical training, dismounted drill, tent pitching, interior guard duty, map reading, tables of organization for signal, infantry, and cavalry units, and horse riding.

TELEGRAPHY CLASS, 1918. The Signal Corps faced an urgent need for telegraphers and radio operators in France during World War I. Camp Alfred Vail offered a six-week intensive course on foreign codes and languages. The U.S. Army first sent 223 men to the camp for training as German-speaking personnel. Additional groups of 50 or more arrived each month thereafter. Camp Alfred Vail trained a total of 2,416 enlisted men and 448 officers for war in 1917.

STORAGE BATTERY CHARGING PLANT. Power during this time came from dry cell batteries, storage batteries, or generators. The majority of storage batteries used by the Signal Corps consisted of two cells. In order to protect the cells against damage, they were enclosed in a strong wooden box at the top of which terminals for connections were provided. Special care had to be taken with storage of the batteries to prevent acid leaking or spilling.

STENOGRAPHERS AND MAIL CLERKS. Civilian stenographers comprised a significant percentage of the radio laboratory personnel at Camp Alfred Vail. A shortage of stenographers during World War I necessitated recruiting posters to target them. These advertised good salaries, opportunities for promotion, and the satisfaction of doing one's part to defeat the kaiser. The salary for a stenographer was advertised at $1,100 a year.

GARAGE FOR THE RADIO LABORATORIES. The Signal Corps Radio Laboratories existed from the time of the post's inception until 1929, when they were renamed the Signal Corps Laboratories. The laboratory prior to 1929 focused on designing and testing radio sets and field wire equipment. Although overshadowed by the Signal School, the radio laboratory was one of the most important facilities at Fort Monmouth.

QUARTERS OF TELEPHONE OPERATORS, CAMP ALFRED VAIL. In October 1916, the office of the chief signal officer asked the executives of American Telephone and Telegraph (AT&T), Western Electric, Western Union, and the Postal Telegraph Company to recruit from among their trained employees personnel for a signal-enlisted reserve corps. The response was more than could have been hoped for when 1,400 of the 6,000 male employees of the Bell Telephone Company of Pennsylvania, an AT&T subsidiary, applied for enlistment.

COMPANY STOCKROOM. This photograph shows a soldier unpacking a recent delivery of shirts, gloves, and hats for the company stockroom. The box is stamped "96 lbs., the Camp Ordnance Officer, Camp Alfred Vail, Little Silver, New Jersey, Depot Stores. From Watervliet G.S.O. Depot." The Watervliet Arsenal in Albany County, New York, was established in 1813. The general supply ordnance depot, or GSO depot, supplied training camps in the surrounding states with everything from rifles to clothes.

PVT. ERNEST C. STRUBLE, 1917.
Pvt. Ernest C. Struble was a member
of Company C, 10th Field Signal
Battalion, Camp Alfred Vail. This
battalion returned to the United
States on June 27, 1919, having served
with distinction during World War I.
A memorial at Fort Monmouth
honors E. Frederic Wright (March 12,
1899–April 30, 1974), the founder of the
10th Signal Battalion Association and
the Seventh Division Association of
World War One Veterans.

SOLDIER OPERATES A SWITCHBOARD. This soldier is participating in a field-training exercise
in the wilds of Camp Alfred Vail in November 1918. Between August 1917 and October 1918,
the American Expeditionary Force (AEF) in France received five telegraph battalions, two field
signal battalions, one depot battalion, and an aero construction squadron trained at Camp
Alfred Vail.

COOKS PREPARE EVENING MEAL. Kitchens were located as far as possible from places of slaughter and other refuse areas. The U.S. Army procured fresh meats, fish, dairy products, and vegetables for training camps in the United States. During World War I when perishable food was not available, troops were provided with emergency rations that often consisted of roast or corned beef, sardines, bread, coffee, and cigarettes.

ENLISTED MESS HALL. Specific hours were designated for meals. Soldiers lined up to enter the mess hall and then lined up again to wash their mess gear after eating. The U.S. Army had established schools for cooking and baking in 1905, and cooks often used recipes from military cookbooks. An individual field mess kit included a skillet or meat can made of aluminum, a canteen cup, a knife, a fork, and a spoon.

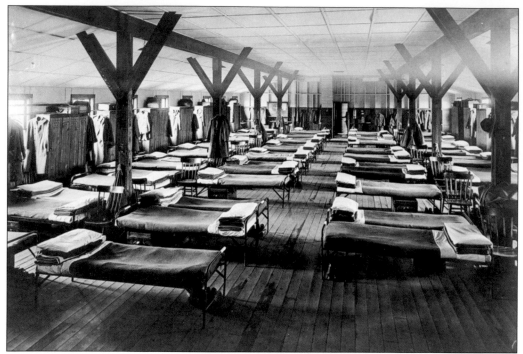

ENLISTED MEN'S BARRACKS. Col. James B. Allison initiated plans for the construction of permanent barracks in 1925. Four redbrick barracks were completed in August 1927 around what is now known as Barker Circle. These housed approximately 200 men each. Quarters for field officers, company officers, and noncommissioned officers were completed in August 1928. These constituted the second and third increments of permanent construction. The remaining permanent construction occurred in the 1930s.

CAMP ALFRED VAIL ALL-STARS, 1922. Recreation was an integral part of early camp life. Sports played an important part in conditioning post personnel as well as providing them with entertainment and relaxation. Football opponents included the Freehold Bears, West Point enlisted men, Fort Hancock, and Governor's Island. Sports headlines from this time period include "Fort Monmouth attack riddles West Point enlisted men, 27-0" and "Monmouth takes Hancock, 27 to 0."

Two

PIGEON TRAINING TO RADAR MOON BOUNCE

FORT MONMOUTH OFFICERS, C. 1926. During 1922, the officers' division reorganized its courses into two main sections: a company officers' course for Signal Corps officers and a basic course in signal subjects for officers of other arms and services and for newly commissioned Signal Corps officers. Both sections lasted nine months.

PIGEON LOFTS, C. 1920. The successful use of homing pigeons in World War I prompted the U.S. Army to perpetuate the service after the armistice. Maj. Gen. George O. Squier established the Signal Corps Pigeon Breeding and Training section at Camp Alfred Vail in 1919. The fort received 150 pairs of breeders, which resided together with some of the hero pigeons of the war in one fixed and 14 mobile lofts. Ray R. Delhauer directed the section from 1919 to 1925.

LINEMEN INSTRUCTION AT THE SIGNAL SCHOOL. Linemen maintained telephone and telegraph lines. This was considered a very hazardous job due to the inherent risk of electrocution. ROTC training at many universities included pole-climbing instruction for telephone electricians.

MAKING METEOROLOGICAL OBSERVATIONS. The fort has had a long history with innovative meteorological experiments, beginning in the early 1920s. The first radio-equipped weather balloon was launched at Fort Monmouth in 1928. This was the first major development in the application of electronics to the study of weather and of conditions in the upper atmosphere.

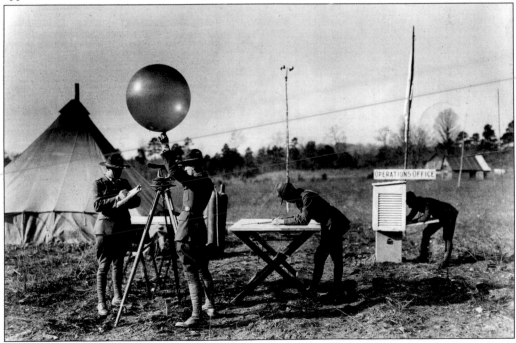

METEOROLOGICAL EXPERIMENTS. The Signal Corps Engineering Laboratories at Fort Monmouth developed, among other things, the standard military anemometer for measuring wind speed and the first military portable weather station.

MOTION PICTURE THEATER. One of the airplane hangars served as the war department motion picture theater in the 1920s and 1930s. The movie posters shown here include *Cimarron*, a western directed by Wesley Ruggles and starring Richard Dix and Irene Dunne. The film won three Oscars, including best picture, in 1931. The other film featured is *Kiki*, a musical directed by Sam Taylor. This film starred Mary Pickford and Reginald Denny.

SIGNAL CORPS HEAT DETECTORS. This heat detector received directional data from radio equipment (part of one antenna may be seen at the right) and in turn controlled the pointing of a searchlight. Col. William R. Blair proved that radar was capable of detecting and measuring the speed of aircraft through a combined system of heat and radio pulse-echo detection. He demonstrated this in May 1937 in front of senior military and congressional officials.

RADAR SET SCR-268. One of the most important pieces of equipment developed during the 1930s was radar (radio detection and ranging). The term refers to the equipment itself as well as the method by which distant or invisible objects can be detected by reflected radio waves. Blair holds the patent for the first American radar, Signal Corps radio (SCR) 268, developed and tested at Fort Monmouth.

PIGEON SERVICE VEHICLE. Fort Monmouth's pigeon handlers successfully bred and trained birds capable of flying under the cover of darkness in 1928. By the outset of World War II, they had also perfected techniques for training two-way pigeons. The first test was conducted in May 1941. Twenty birds completed the approximately 28-mile round-trip from Fort Monmouth to Freehold in half an hour.

MOBILE PIGEON LOFT, 1930S. Trainers separated breeders and racers in the loft as well as cocks and hens at certain times. It took several days to home a pigeon so it would know where to return to its loft. For that reason, lofts were usually located at a U.S. Army headquarters because the location was stable. The home loft could also be a moving vehicle during combat operations.

THOMASON ACT OFFICERS, 1939–1940. The Thomason Act was an act of Congress that allowed selected ROTC graduates to serve a year in the regular army. Qualified reserve officers received a permanent commission in the regular army at the end of that year. Officers commissioned through this act were known as "Tommies." R. E. Thomason was a member of the House of Representatives from the 16th district of Texas.

32

UNIDENTIFIED SOLDIER WITH THE BLAIR RADIOSONDE. This radiosonde was one of the earliest developed by Col. William R. Blair around 1930 at the Signal Corps Laboratories. A radiosonde is a small radio transmitter that transmits information on temperature, pressure, direction, and speed of wind and humidity as it rises. Altogether, Blair held 11 patents. This included one for the radio-meteorograph, a forerunner to the modern radiosonde.

VEHICLE RADIO, 1930s. The Signal Corps had experimented with radios in vehicles during the war with Mexico in 1916, but they were not very successful, as the rugged terrain often hampered transmissions. Then in the early 1930s, personnel developed the SCR-194 and 195. These radios could be used in a vehicle and had a range of five miles. The development of FM radio meant that vehicle radios were finally a reality.

COMMANDER'S QUARTERS, C. 1930. This commander's quarters was a 4,536-square-foot structure on Riverside Avenue. It was a preexisting house bought by the U.S. Army along with the 400-area parcel of the installation. The main building was 24 feet by 63 feet, and the wings were 17 feet by 18 feet. Awnings, a gas hot water heater, and a stoker electric furnace were added in the early 1930s. It was demolished in July 1936.

OFFICERS' ROW, 1936. Officer housing is located north of Greely Field lining Russel and Allen Avenues and surrounded by a landscaped open space known today as Voris Park. Officer housing includes single-family dwellings constructed for field officers and duplex family dwellings constructed for company officers. The duplex units are symmetrical, eight-bay buildings with paired, central main entries. Each has a gabled, pedimented surround.

WORKS PROGRESS ADMINISTRATION CONSTRUCTION, SQUIER HALL. The final phase of the prewar permanent construction program at Fort Monmouth ended between 1934 and 1936 under the Works Progress Administration (WPA). WPA workers completed the fire station, guardhouse, and Signal Corps Laboratory (Squier Hall) in 1935, as well as three sets of quarters for field officers and three sets for company-grade officers. A blacksmith shop, incinerator, bakery, warehouses, band barracks, and utility shops were completed in 1934.

STUDENT OFFICERS, THE SIGNAL CORPS SCHOOL, 1938–1939. The Signal Corps School, the name of which had changed to the Signal School in 1921 to reflect its mission at that time, reverted to its original name as part of a reorganization in 1935. As World War II approached, the Signal Corps School functioned with three distinct divisions: the officers' department, the enlisted department, and the department of training literature.

PARADE, 1941. World War II led to a sizable expansion at Fort Monmouth. The U.S. Army acquired the Charles Wood area in 1942 for the Signal Corps Replacement Center. Construction was completed within 90 days on 60 barracks, 8 mess halls, 19 school buildings, 10 administration buildings, a recreation hall, a post exchange, an infirmary, and a chapel. The U.S. Army also leased additional land at various sites in Monmouth and Ocean Counties.

SIGNAL CORPS LABORATORIES PERSONNEL, 1934. The Signal Corps Electrical Laboratory, the Signal Corps Meteorological Laboratory, and the Signal Corps Laboratory at the Bureau of Standards (all in Washington, D.C.) moved to Fort Monmouth in 1929 in the interest of economy and efficiency. Conjointly, these laboratories became known as the Signal Corps Laboratories. These laboratories developed radar in 1937 and the first FM backpack radio in 1941.

SIGNAL CORPS LABORATORY METAL SHOP PERSONNEL, 1945. From left to right are (first row) Dorothy Bacon, unidentified, Axel Christensen, Robert Weiss, Captain Broms, Thomas L. Parker, Fred Van Dorn, and Anastasia Sirutus; (second row) John Bates, Andrew Larsen, Henry Lorkewicz, Fred Vroom, John Walsh, Harry Hutchinson, and Charles Wendt; (third row) Charles Summers, Howard Douglas, Martin Schmidt, Oscar Tampier, Elmer Applegate, and John Feeney.

CAMP EVANS POLICE OFFICERS. Pictured from left to right are officers Zurst, Anglin, Johns, Supeski, and McCall in October 1942. Fort Monmouth has at various times in its history employed military police, often called provost marshals, as well as civilian Department of Defense police. These personnel have been responsible for various types of law enforcement duties on the installation. The Military Police Corps was established as a permanent branch of the U.S. Army in 1941.

COMPANY F, 15TH SIGNAL SERVICE REGIMENT, 1942. This signal regiment traces its origins to the 15th Service Company organized at Camp Alfred Vail in 1919. The company grew to regiment size during the war years, and in April 1943, the 15th Student Training Regiment was assigned and replaced the 15th Signal Service Regiment. The regiment was disbanded at Fort Monmouth on May 31, 1945.

PRODUCTION AND DRAFTING GROUP, CAMP EVANS, 1943. The production and drafting group designed new equipment and redesigned and altered existing equipment. The group was first organized on December 1, 1942. It completed all manufacturing drawings for Signal Corps equipment, drew engineering sketches as required, and worked on production design problems with the engineering branches. It also maintained drafting supplies. (Courtesy of Infoage.)

COMPANY D, 14TH SIGNAL SERVICE REGIMENT (PROVISIONAL). This regiment was activated at Fort Monmouth on April 11, 1942, and disbanded on July 15, 1942. It consisted of a headquarters company, student companies A–T inclusive (except for J and N), plus a fixed radio station company. The regiment was created per Special Orders No. 96, Headquarters Fort Monmouth. Upon disbandment, the unit's personnel and equipment transferred to the 15th Signal Service Regiment.

NEW JERSEY GOVERNOR WALTER EDGE VISIT. Gov. Walter Edge visited Fort Monmouth and attended a review in his honor in the summer of 1944. From left to right are Col. James B. Haskell, Edge, and Brig. Gen. George L. Van Deusen. Van Deusen was the 11th commanding officer in 1941 and 1942. He concurrently served as commandant of the Signal Corps School. Haskell was the 12th commanding officer of Fort Monmouth from 1942 to 1944.

GOLDEN GLOVES BANQUET, 15TH SIGNAL REGIMENT, 1940S. The Golden Gloves was an annual amateur boxing competition in the United States. The competition received its name because of the miniature golden glove that was given to the winner. The competition began in the 1920s in New York and Chicago and quickly spread to other cities. Army personnel regularly competed in these tournaments.

SOLDIERS TRAINING, WORLD WAR II ERA. Soldiers wearing headsets sit at mechanical typewriters. Several different companies manufactured these headsets during World War II, including Western Electric and Cannon Ball Empire. Troops in the field often used portable Corona, Remington, and Underwood typewriters. Civilians had to get special permission to buy typewriters during the war, as the military requisitioned all available models. Just as civilians were urged to sell cameras to the Signal Corps, civilians were also encouraged to donate typewriters to the military.

TELEPHONE IN A JEEP. Sgt. Neil Hull studies a map in a test maneuver at Fort Monmouth as Pfc. Donald Keer reports positions with the new combat radio telephone. This experimental system, developed by the U.S. Army Signal Corps Research and Development Laboratory, allowed on-the-move telephone service for scouting missions and frontline communications. A dozen or more jeeps could be linked in such a wireless telephone network with a central switchboard in a light truck.

UNIDENTIFIED PERSONNEL, PROJECT CIRRUS, C. 1947. Fort scientists tackled the old admonition "Everybody talks about the weather, but nobody does anything about it." These scientists, together with scientists from the navy, air force, and General Electric, developed the ability to manipulate weather by seeding clouds with silver iodide and dry ice. Ten Signal Corps photographers covered the project. Some reports indicate the technology was used effectively for clearing away cloud cover in Vietnam.

Dr. Walter McAfee and Col. Thomas K. Trigg at the Diana Radar Site. This Belmar (later Wall Township) site witnessed a milestone in scientific history on January 10, 1946. Under the direction of Lt. Col. John J. DeWitt, a specially designed radar antenna called the Diana Tower successfully bounced electronic signals off the moon. Dr. Walter McAfee performed the mathematical calculations for the project. Newspaper reports put the feat into the same category as the development of the atomic bomb.

Arctic Test Chamber. One of the important aspects of communications-electronics equipment development is testing the systems under specific atmospheric conditions. In the Signal Corps Engineering Laboratories, electronic equipment acclimated to the particular conditions in arctic and tropical chambers. The Climatic Test Laboratory created snow conditions by introducing minute ice crystals into a region containing super-cooled water droplets, creating a super-cooled cloud.

Three

McCarthy to the Space Race

Sen. Joseph McCarthy, Camp Evans, 1953. Fort Monmouth entered perhaps the darkest period of its history at the end of the Korean War, when it was for a time the object of congressional scrutiny and public notoriety. Sen. Joseph McCarthy launched an inquiry on August 31, 1953, designed to prove that Julius Rosenberg created a spy ring at Fort Monmouth. Forty-two employees lost their jobs on mere suspicion; they were later reinstated.

LISTENING TO SIGNALS. Personnel are listening to signals from the Explorer satellite. Explorer I was the first United States earth satellite launched from Cape Canaveral on January 31, 1958. The fort's Deal Test Area monitored satellites and was for a period one of the prime tracking stations of the North Atlantic Missile Range. When Sputnik I was launched in 1957, the Deal site was the first government installation in the country to detect and record the signals.

CAMERA SET AN/PFH-2, 1954. This 100-inch-long range camera was dubbed the "Peeping Tom." Pfc. Jim R. Sarver (foreground) sights through the terrestrial telescope peep sight as Pfc. Robert Ayres clicks the shutter at the camera back. Developed at Fort Monmouth, this camera could knife through atmospheric haze up to 30 miles to record battlefront objectives. The camera was considered such a breakthrough that it was featured on the *Today* show.

COMPUTER TRAINING, LATE 1950S OR EARLY 1960S. Fort Monmouth was at the cutting edge of computer development. A mobile digital computer (MOBIDIC) developed here in 1960 was the world's first mobile, van-mounted computer for use at field army and theater levels. This computer was the first experiment in automating combat support functions and was the prototype of the computers the U.S. Army used in Vietnam to automate artillery, surveillance, logistics, and battlefield administration.

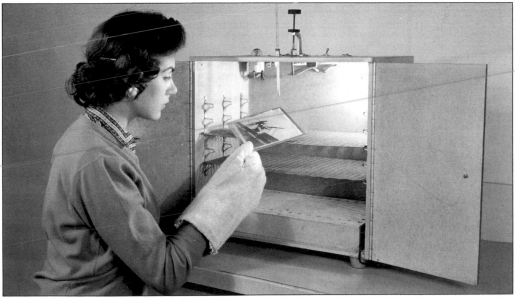

PLASTIC PHOTOGRAPHY, 1956. The enlisted men's division of the Signal Corps School at Fort Monmouth (1919–1976) originally included the photography department. The post built laboratory facilities for the course in 1926. During the Korean War, Fort Monmouth continued to offer photography classes. In 1966, Congress authorized construction of three new permanent classroom buildings to accommodate an influx of students during the Vietnam conflict. This included building 814 for the photographic laboratory.

GAS CELL BATTERY, 1959. Dr. Werner Von Braun, chief scientist of the U.S. Army's missile program, inspects the gas cell battery under study at the U.S. Army Signal Corps Research and Development Laboratory. Arthur Daniel, left, explains how the battery converts hydrogen and oxygen to electrical power directly. Looking on is Leonard Rokaw, chief of technical information at the laboratory. Von Braun's visit included a tour of the space electronics facilities.

PLASMA RESEARCH, 1950S. Dr. Rudolph G. Buser, right, aims a radio signal through plasma to instruments operated by his associate Paul H. Wolfert. The experiment simulates the plasma interference between two spaceships. The plasma shown here is a form of electrically charged matter that fills the earth's ionosphere. Plasma can greatly distort and reflect radio waves. Under certain conditions, it could even cause a radio blackout that would cut off communications.

MINIATURE MAGNETRON TUBE.
Joan Conran, U.S. Army Signal
Corps Engineering Laboratories
employee, compares the size of a
new miniature magnetron tube
developed by the Signal Corps at
Fort Monmouth with an ordinary
golf ball. Weighing a mere three
ounces, the tiny tube was 50 times
more powerful than the klystron
tube it replaced. The tube was
expected to be of important
military value in short-range
communications between
advanced lines and rear echelons.

**OBSERVING AN EXPERIMENTAL
PYRISTOR.** Army physicist
Joseph Mandelkorn observes an
experimental pyristor through
a magnifying glass as the new
electronic device operates at red
heat in an evacuated chamber.
The device, which shows
marked transistor properties,
worked successfully as a diode
at 1,500 degrees Fahrenheit at
the U.S. Army Signal Corps
Research and Development
Laboratory. Few, if any, electronic
parts could withstand such heat.
This discovery was considered
a major research breakthrough
in electronics.

PROJECT SCORE. Four of the men in the U.S. Army Signal Corps Research and Development Laboratory who worked on Project SCORE (signal communication by orbiting relay equipment) were members of the 88 Club. The 88 Club was a group of scientists from various government agencies involved in the project. From left to right, Marshall Davis, Herbert Hawkins, John Cittadino, and Samuel P. Brown review the operation in chalk. SCORE broadcast the human voice across space via the world's first communications satellite. That voice belonged to Pres. Dwight D. Eisenhower.

ASTRO OBSERVATION CENTER, DEAL, 1959. The U.S. Army Signal Corps Research and Development Laboratory established an astro-electronics division within the communications department in 1958 to give proper recognition and priority to astro-electronics projects. The division included astro-instrumentation, astro-observation and analysis, and astro-communications branches. The observation center was responsible for, among other things, monitoring and tracking satellites. Dr. Werner Von Braun visited the Astro Observation Center in 1959.

DEMONSTRATING NEW FIELD WIRE. This new Signal Corps field wire could be laid at speeds of up to 120 miles per hour by airplanes and was used successfully in Korea. The wire provided a talk range of approximately 12.5 miles.

WALKIE-TALKIE AN/PRC-10. Pfc. Clayton T. Coleman demonstrates use of the walkie-talkie AN/PRC-10 in 1951. A radio receiver-transmitter, case, carrying harness, antenna, handset, belt suspenders, and combat belt comprised the radio set. Except for frequency range, the AN/PRC-10 was identical to the AN/PRC-8 and AN/PRC-9. They were used in Korea and Vietnam as squad radios. The radios were replaced by the AN/PRC-25, or "prick 25," as it was called.

NIGHT HAWK PHOTO RECONNAISSANCE SYSTEM. This system gave commanders accurate low-level aerial photographs of enemy territory during the hours of darkness. This system combined a new lightweight, rugged camera and an automatic flare ejector with a small radio-controlled RP-71 pilotless aircraft. The photographic branch of the laboratories' components department designed and developed the 15-pound KA-28 camera, which Fairchild Camera and Instrument Corporation of Syosset, New York, built. Anthony B. Orefice was the project engineer.

DEPARTMENT OF NONRESIDENT INSTRUCTION. Pictured from left to right are Capt. Florence M. Belknap, Frank Mohler, and Capt. Gene H. Hawisher at work in the administration office around 1952. This department of the Signal School provided long-distance instruction for nonresident students. Approximately 50 personnel administered the nonresident courses. The average enrollment during this period was about 120 students per month. The Signal Corps Publications Agency prepared texts and manuals.

THE BREEZE BUSTER. This weather gun could aim and hit itself with a round-trip bullet to measure low-altitude wind velocity. Officially designated the "shooting sphere anemometer," the Breeze Buster could be used under poor visibility conditions and could measure the velocity of gale-force winds. The idea of adapting the shooting-sphere wind measurement technique for military field conditions originated with Abraham Arnold and was developed and tested by Walter Conover, physicists in the laboratories' meteorological branch.

FOREIGN VISIT. Maj. Gen. Kirk B. Lawton hosts a visit from the Royal Australian Corps of Signal on July 26, 1952. From its earliest days, Fort Monmouth has played host to a myriad of foreign military visitors to share knowledge, demonstrate new systems, negotiate the sale of equipment, and discuss areas for collaboration. Today the fort has five foreign liaison officers from Australia, Canada, France, Germany, and Israel assigned to the research and development center.

SOUND RECORDING CAMERA PH-270. Pfc. Bernard McBride explains the PH-270 operation to cadets of the United States Military Academy during their visit on June 7, 1952. Pfc. Edgar Schuller, right, is operating the recorder PH-271. The camera and recorder took motion pictures and recorded sound simultaneously on the same film. The 35-millimeter film was used by newsreel and motion picture assignment units throughout the armed forces.

TENT DARKROOM PH-392. Pfc. Robert Nelson, instructor in the photograph division of the Signal School (wearing a khaki shirt), is shown as he orients cadets on the components and use of the PH-392. This tent darkroom consisted of 35 square feet of floor space for photographic and darkroom equipment and stood six feet high. Eastman Kodak manufactured the tent, which allowed still pictures to be produced by these mobile units close to the front lines.

CELEBRATING THE 96TH ANNIVERSARY OF THE SIGNAL CORPS, 1956. M.Sgt. Edward F. Martin, 75, the oldest soldier on active duty in the U.S. Army, and Pvt. Lee R. Biddulph, 17, the youngest Signal Corps soldier, view the old and new in radio equipment. At Martin's left is a radio set SCR-54, the type used during World War I. Biddulph is holding a hand-held radio used by the U.S. Army in the 1950s.

TACTICAL TELEVISION CAMERA, 1956. This eight-pound tactical television camera pointed by Pvt. Craig Heatley, right, and the handy walkie-talkie radio operated by Pvt. William Fitzgerald served as reconnaissance eyes and ears. The television camera had built-in batteries, freeing the cameraman for the first time from the cumbersome cable connections of earlier models. The Signal Corps Engineering Laboratories developed this latest combat aid, which the Radio Corporation of America built.

DEMONSTRATING G-STRING SURFACE WAVE TRANSMISSION. Dr. George Gaubau checks instruments telling him how the G-string surface wave transmission line is operating in December 1952. This photograph was taken at the Coles Signal Laboratory in Red Bank. G-string is used with high-frequency communications sets.

RADIO SET AN/GRC-53 (SERVICE TEST). The Westinghouse Electric Company manufactured this four-voice radio relay terminal for the U.S. Army Signal Corps Research and Development Laboratory in 1959. The equipment shown here is mounted in a quarter-ton truck to demonstrate its use in a tactical environment. The AN/VRC-87 vehicular short-range radio later replaced this system.

MOTION PICTURE SCHOOL PHOTOGRAPHERS, 1953. Pfc. William Ryan, far left, is pictured with unidentified members of motion picture class No. 159. They used Bell and Howell Filmo 16-millimeter cameras. The photograph was taken in the 800 area of Fort Monmouth where barracks buildings had been converted into classrooms and offices for the photography school. Training in photography was offered at Camp Alfred Vail as early as 1919.

EXPLAINING THE ATOMIC DEMONSTRATOR. Cpl. Donald Lunn, training aids branch, explains the intricacies of the atomic demonstrator to Jean Fitzgerald, civilian employee of the Signal Corps Publications Agency, and Cpt. Russell Krueger, who is holding Russell Jr. This system was a part of the training aids exhibit during Fort Monmouth Day, Armed Forces Week, on May 15, 1950.

STAFF OF THE COMMAND AND GENERAL STAFF SCHOOL. The staff of the Command and General Staff School are, from left to right, Lt. Col. Gregory C. Lee, Lt. Col. Lewis W. Whittemore, Col. Emanual M. Kline, Col. Harry E. Besley, Col. Loeser M. Boskey, Col. Rendle H. Fussell, and Lt. Col. Jacob H. Herzog. The last graduation of the Command and General Staff School to be held in this country under U.S. Army area supervision was at the Signal Corps School on March 2, 1957.

SIGNAL CORPS 90TH ANNIVERSARY. Members of the reception line at Gibbs Hall pose prior to greeting guests at the anniversary dinner dance in 1953. From left to right are Maj. Gen. and Mrs. K. B. Lawton, Maj. Gen. and Mrs. G. I. Back, Katherine Mauborgne, Maj. Gen. G. E. Van Deusen (Ret.) and Effie Van Deusen, Brig. Gen. and Mrs. W. T. Guest, Brig. Gen. and Virginia Corderman, and Brig. Gen. and Mrs. E. R. Petzing.

AIDES DE CAMP, GIBBS HALL. Aides de camp to generals attending the Signal Corps anniversary dinner pose for a picture at the officers' club on March 3, 1953. The aides de camp are all wearing the distinctive aiguillette, a braided gold cord worn on the left shoulder. Aides appointed for general officers usually serve a tour of two years.

OTTO MEYER AND BRIG. GEN. RICHARD HORNE. Otto Meyer was the resident pigeon expert at Fort Monmouth after World War II. He was called up in 1941 and took command of the Army Pigeon Service Agency in 1943. In this position, he was responsible for pigeon training all over the world, including 3,000 handlers. In 1947, he became the technical adviser of the Fort Monmouth Pigeon Breeding and Training Center to further develop and perfect the art.

CARDINAL SPELLMAN WITH FORT OFFICERS. Here are Maj. Gen. Francis Lanahan and Francis Cardinal Spellman with officers and enlisted men outside Company F mess hall in May 1950. From left to right are Col. J. D. O'Connell, deputy president of the Signal Corps board; post chaplain Maj. Joseph "Father Joe" Chmielewski; Spellman, archbishop of New York; Lanahan, commanding general of Fort Monmouth; and an unidentified enlisted man.

VAN KIRK MEMORIAL BENCH. Van Kirk Park was designated in 1943 and is located between Brewer and Malterer Avenues. First Lt. John Stewart Van Kirk died in combat on November 30, 1942, in Djedeida, Tunisia. He had previously attended officer candidate school at Fort Monmouth. A memorial granite bench was erected at Van Kirk Park without ceremony in the early 1950s pursuant to the wishes of his father, the donor.

HANGAR ONE, FEBRUARY 1950. The audience listens to Maj. Gen. Joseph O. Mauborgne during a ceremony for the removal of Hangar One. The old airplane hangars had outlived their useful life by the 1950s. They had been used for various purposes after the aviation mission left Fort Monmouth, including as laboratories and classrooms. Mauborgne was chief signal officer from 1937 to 1941 and a 30-year resident of Little Silver.

HANGAR ONE SIGN. This sign still stands at the entrance to the old aviation area off Oceanport Avenue. Before and after its service as an airfield, the site functioned as a polo field. The last of the hangars was razed in 1983. Known as the 400 area, it is home to various program management offices and garrison-related functions today.

ARMED FORCES WEEK EXHIBIT, MAY 1950. Armed Forces Week included days devoted to the Armed Forces Communications Association (AFCA), Fort Monmouth, the First Army, the north Jersey Shore, Governor's Day, and College Day. Exhibits showcased during the week included those from the U.S. Army Pictorial Service, Signal Corps Training Aids, Signal Corps Historical Exhibit, radio station K2USA, the Signal School, Signal Corps Engineering Laboratories, Signal Patent Agency, Signal Corps Publications Agency, and the Armed Services Electro Standards Agency.

RAWIN DISPLAY, MAY 1950. The Rawin Display attracts the attention of guests. This automatic radio direction finder was designed to obtain meteorological data. It automatically tracked a balloon-borne radiosonde to altitudes of 100,000 feet over distances of 125 miles, providing azimuth and elevation data. The information provided aided pilots and navigators in choosing favorable altitudes for flight and helped ground artillery units in making gun corrections for atmospheric effects on the trajectory of projectiles.

SPECTATORS WATCH MOCK ATTACK. The wife and two sons of Master Sergeant Lowe of Gosslin Avenue show extreme fright during the demonstration of a mock attack on AFCA day, May 13, 1950. The AFCA day events included a wire-laying contest where World War II methods were demonstrated alongside new developments. There was also a demonstration of wire laying by bazooka and helicopters, an air-sea rescue demonstration, communications in combat, and air-to-ground television.

GUESTS VIEW PARADE. Spectators gathered to watch the review of troops on Armed Forces Day, May, 20 1950. Guests were shown two films, *Science in the Signal Corps* and *Alaskan Communication System*. Guests passing through the Signal School exhibit were presented with a certificate attesting to the fact they graduated from the "Blitz Course" of the Signal School. Other popular displays included a snow village, a tropical test box, and guided missiles.

ARMSTRONG HALL DEDICATION. The 389th U.S. Army band plays at the dedication of the Signal Corps museum as Armstrong Hall on May 31, 1955. The building (551) is currently home to various personnel and education offices. The building was named in honor of Maj. Edwin Howard Armstrong, a scientist and Signal Corps soldier. Armstrong held the patent for FM radio and allowed the free use of his patents by the U.S. Army during World War II.

SIGNAL CORPS MUSEUM, MAY 31, 1955. From left to right are Harry Houck, president of the Electronic Measurements Company in New York; Maj. Gen. Victor A. Conrad, commanding general of Fort Monmouth; and Maj. Gen. James D. O'Connell, chief signal officer, assembled for the dedication of the museum as Armstrong Hall. Conrad became the 18th commanding officer of Fort Monmouth in September 1954.

Four

NIGHT VISION TO WEATHER FORECASTING

NIGHT OBSERVATION DEVICE, MAY 21, 1968. This device was the largest and had the greatest range of any of the family of sights developed by the U.S. Army Electronics Command's Night Vision Laboratory. Mounted independent of a weapon on the ground or on a standing tripod, this device was used to detect the presence or activity of an enemy in faint sky glow, moonlight, or starlight at distances up to 1,200 meters.

NIGHT VISION FOR CREW-SERVED WEAPONS. This night vision device was used primarily with the 50-caliber machine gun and was adaptable to a wide range of other weapons, including the Vulcan Air Defense System and the 106-millimeter recoilless rifle. Weighing in at 16 pounds with a range of 1,000 meters, it could intensify starlight, moonlight, or a faint sky glow within its viewing area to give soldiers near-daylight vision at night.

AN/PPS-6 GROUND SURVEILLANCE RADAR, 1962. This radar was a small lightweight, ground-to-ground surveillance radar used to detect moving personnel and vehicles in the forward battle area, day and night, in all weather conditions. Weighing in at 35 pounds, it was the first radar of its kind, light enough to be transported and operated by a single soldier. A team of engineers headed by Harold Tate conceived, designed, and built the set.

RADIO DIRECTION FINDING EQUIPMENT. Second Lt. Robert Gregg explains the operation of radio direction finder PRD-1 to North Atlantic Treaty Organization (NATO) officers attending an electronic warfare course at the U.S. Army Signal Center and School at Fort Monmouth in 1962. A loop antenna, a superheterodyne-type receiver, and a power supply unit comprised this mobile and portable direction finder. It could determine the direction of enemy or friendly radio signals.

TACTICAL AVIONICS SYSTEM SIMULATOR FACILITY. The overall view of this facility shows the consoles that comprised the tactical avionics system simulator (TASS), which included a large-scale computer system and two maneuverable cockpits. TASS simulated the in-flight performance of the electronic systems used in U.S. Army tactical aircraft and was used to evaluate aviation electronics during the design stage. Assistant U.S. Army secretary Willis M. Hawkins unveiled the facility, located in the Albert J. Myer Center, on December 13, 1965.

TELEPHONE REPEATER AN/TCC-11. S.Sgt. Dana P. Farris, left, and Specialist 5th Class Charles Cox use a test set to check the unattended wire repeater AN/TCC-11 in December 1961. The AN/TCC-11 was a four-wire, unattended carrier telephone repeater. It was used to extend the length of a 12-channel, spiral-four carrier telephone system that used telephone terminals AN/TCC-7 and attended telephone repeaters AN/TCC-8. The extension obtained for each TCC-11 added to the system was five and three-quarters miles.

SATELLITE COMMUNICATIONS TEST OPERATIONS CENTER, 1963. M.Sgt. Lex Utter points out oscilloscope pattern relationships to telemetry circuits activating the display board, shown here behind Sgt. 1st Class Theodore Condon (kneeling) and S.Sgt. Kenton Bishop in the satellite Communications Test Operations Center. The men are participating in a training program designed to provide competent personnel for operating and maintaining all surface facilities of the US. Army Satellite Communications Agency.

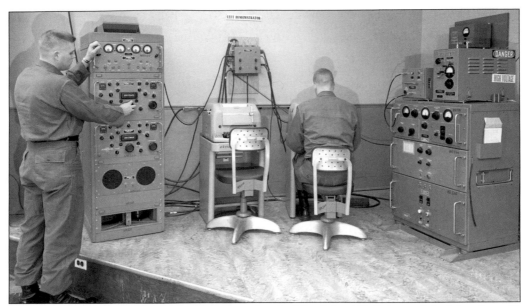

RADIO SET AN/GRC-26D. From left to right, 2nd Lt. John W. Rider and 2nd Lt. Peter E. Meyer study the operation of radio set AN/GRC-26D. The "ANGRY 26," as it was known, was a shelter-mounted high-frequency radio teletypewriter communications system. It could operate from mobile, moveable, and fixed locations. The SCR-399 mobile high-frequency radio set was modernized and equipped with a teletype apparatus. The new model with this modernization was designated AN/GRC-26.

EXPLAINING RADIO RECEIVER OPERATION. Capt. Robert A. Denney explains this radio receiver to, from left to right, Lt. J. S. K. Agbemnu, Capt. Ralph A. Koch, Lt. E. A. Erskine, and Capt. Jerry D. Lambo at the U.S. Army Signal Corps School.

U.S. ARMY'S SUPER DETECTOR, 1960. Pvt. Henry Hahlbohm of Long Island City, New York, listens to a signal picked up by a new experimental "ruby maser," a device that was pound for pound the most sensitive detector in the history of science. Hughes Aircraft Company and the Signal Corps developed the maser, which could increase the range of important military communications and radar systems tenfold.

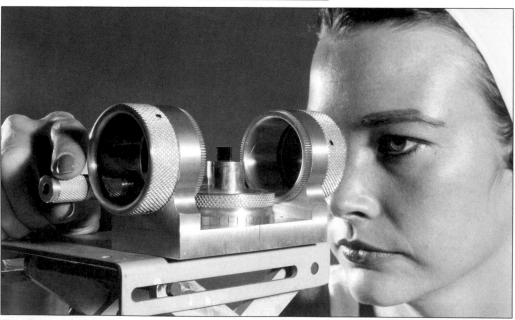

THE RUBY MASER. Pictured are ruby, the square, synthetic gem between the lenses, and Shirley Brumfield, who is finding the optic axis of the ruby crystal to determine the frequency at which it will function. The ruby was then drastically cooled within the complete maser to 452 degrees below zero, thus affording such great sensitivity that the amplifier could detect very weak signals from distant stars or space vehicles millions of miles away.

RADAR SET AN/PPS-4. A soldier demonstrates the AN/PPS-4 (transistorized) radar at the U.S. Army Signal Corps Research and Development Laboratory on May 21, 1962. This radar could spot a single enemy moving a half mile away in darkness or fog and could spot vehicles or large groups at a much farther distance. Sperry Gyroscope Company of Great Neck, New York, developed this electronic sentry to convert pinpoint radar signals for easy detection in the observer's headphone.

PREFLIGHT TEST SET AN/ASM-88. Col. Roman T. Ulans, commanding officer of the U.S. Army Electronics Materiel Support Agency (USA EMSA), is at the controls of an H-13 helicopter. He was briefed on the operation of the AN/ASM-88 by Radio Corporation of America engineer Roger Plaisted at Monmouth County Airport, where the set was undergoing evaluation tests. The set was used in preflight checking of electronic communication and navigation devices on U.S. Army aircraft.

FORECASTING THE WEATHER. Scientists make experimental weather forecasts with the low level meteorological simulator, which makes electronic comparisons between the natural forces of the atmosphere. Here project scientist Abraham Golden, left, looks at the output that is typed out automatically as columns of figures, while Dr. Donald M. Swingle, a laboratory meteorologist, feeds new data into the computer. The Atmospheric Sciences Laboratory designed and developed the equipment.

ARMED FORCES DAY, MONMOUTH MALL, MAY 1967. Armed Forces Day was established in 1949 and designed to replace the individual holidays of each of the services, now consolidated into the Department of Defense. Fort Monmouth has a long history of opening its doors to the public for this important celebration, held on the third Saturday of May each year.

BALLOON INFLATION AND LAUNCHING DEVICE ML-594. A soldier carefully inflates a balloon on April 24, 1964. The ML-594/U was a portable inflation shelter and launching platform designed for use in the field in an inflation and launching system. The device was designed to secure and protect meteorological balloons during inflation and launching.

PROJECT ICECAP. In the 1960s, fort scientists and their counterparts from Denmark gathered in Greenland to participate in Project Icecap. An antenna, specially designed at Fort Monmouth, was mounted in a C-121 constellation flying laboratory and was used for signal transmission by an in-flight radar technique to measure the polar icecaps. The resulting data provided scientists with new information about these regions and insight into how electromagnetic waves traveled through solid substances.

TESTING A NEW LIGHT DEFLECTOR. IBM (International Business Machines Corporation) physicist Dr. Millard A. Habegger is shown testing a new digital light deflector system that could position a light beam to any of 131,072 points at speeds exceeding 100,000 selections per second. IBM developed and delivered the system under contract to the U.S. Army Electronics Command.

MAKING DIAMONDS, MARCH 25, 1960. This powerful hydraulic press was used to make diamonds from ordinary graphite. Diamonds, nature's hardest-known substance, are a form of carbon. In the successful synthesis achieved by the Signal Corps, a graphite and metal charge was subjected to a pressure of 1.25 million pounds per square inch in a two-stage pressure chamber. Here John E. Tydings, a signal laboratory engineer, is preparing a synthesis experiment.

PORTABLE HELMET RADIO. The Signal Corps' helmet radios AN/PRC-34, shown here, were in the experimental stage at this time. Squad leaders of the future were expected to use sets evolved from this idea. Trying out the fully operable sets are cadets Gary E. Crowther, left, and Douglas P. Bennett, members of the West Point class of 1964. The class visited the U.S. Army Signal Corps Research and Development Laboratory during a training trip.

JUNGLE RADIO PROPAGATION RESEARCH, THAILAND. The pachyderm radio, carried on an elephant with the antenna stretched between a lead animal and back to a third animal (from which this picture was taken), achieved considerable communications success when mud and terrain bogged down ordinary transport. Shown here are Frederick H. Dickson, right, scientific director of the U.S. Army Radio Propagation Agency at Fort Monmouth, and contract engineer A. Girratana. The project officer was Howard L. Kitts.

FORT MONMOUTH TRADITION COMMITTEE, 1962. This committee was formerly known as the Signal Corps Tradition Committee. Seated are, from left to right, Maj. Glenn S. Stewart, J. P. Hoffman, Lt. Col. Melvyn W. Fuller, Lt. Col. Ted. J. Palik, Col. R. I. Ulans, Col. Raymond H. Bates (chairman), Col. Murray A. Little (former chairman), Col. Leonard Drazen, Col. Robert C. Barthle, Col. Walter C. Ellis (Ret.), James A. McClung, William M. Myers, and secretary Helen C. Phillips.

COMMUNICATIONS SYSTEMS AGENCY EXHIBIT, 1968. The U.S. Army Communications Systems Agency was located in Squier Hall. The activity handled the acquisition and fielding of information and telecommunications systems in support of the worldwide Defense Communications System. In addition, the activity supported the state and commerce departments, the National Security Agency, the Federal Aviation Administration, and foreign allied governments in improving and modernizing their communications systems.

PRODUCTION ENGINEERING DIVISION, COLES AREA. Here are personnel working in the production engineering division in the late 1960s. Dedicated specialists in production engineering have existed at Fort Monmouth from the time of the Signal Corps Laboratories up until today. Production engineering is devoted to the continuous improvement of systems from early involvement in the design phase to minimize costs and increase efficiency. Prototypes were often made to allow for early identification of problems.

PERSONNEL ENTER NIGHT VISION EXHIBIT. As America geared up for war in Vietnam, Fort Monmouth experts fielded night vision systems that helped individual riflemen perform tasks at night. Second-generation night vision devices (image intensification technology) replaced the first-generation "sniper scope" (near infrared technology) of World War II. The small starlight scope AN/PVS-2, the crew-served weapons sight AN/TVS-2, and the medium-range night observation device AN/TVS-4 all saw service in Vietnam.

CENTENNIAL TIME CAPSULE. The centennial time capsule was installed in a ceremony in front of Russel Hall on September 16, 1960, in honor of the first centennial of the Signal Corps. The capsule will be opened on June 21, 2060. It contains items depicting the status of military communications in 1960, as well as historical material showing the origins of the corps and progress made during its first 100 years.

OPENING THE NEW BOOKSTORE, 1960. Brig. Gen. Charles M. Baer, commandant of the Signal Corps School, is shown making the first purchase at the grand opening of the bookstore. Making the sale is saleswoman Catherine Matches, as Lt. Gordon Page, bookstore officer, looks on. The main store, near the post exchange, was open on Monday, Tuesday, Thursday, and Friday from 10:00 a.m. to 6:00 p.m. and Saturday from 9:00 a.m. to 3:00 p.m.

FAREWELL SALUTE, JUNE 9, 1962. Maj. Gen. Ralph T. Nelson conducts a final review at Greely Field on the occasion of his retirement. Nelson was assigned to Fort Monmouth from December 1947 to June 1949 as an instructor and was later named director of the officers' department at the Signal School. In 1955, he was named chief of staff and deputy post commander. Nelson became the 18th chief signal officer in 1959.

SHOWCASE REVIEW, JUNE 9, 1962. Members of the showcase revue perform at the au revoir dinner held at Gibbs Hall in honor of Maj. Gen. Ralph T. Nelson and Christine Nelson. From left to right are Ginny Usnick, Mary Ann Weis, Frank Lympkin, and Judy Fishman. Post sergeant Maj. W. Good presented Nelson a certificate naming him an honorary sergeant major. This was Nelson's final visit to Fort Monmouth as head of the Signal Corps.

TRUMPETERS PERFORM, GIBBS HALL. The U.S. Army Signal Corps School trumpeters perform at the cocktail party preceding the au revoir dinner for Maj. Gen. Ralph T. Nelson. Nelson retired with more than 34 years of military service. A graduate of West Point in 1928, he died in 1968 and is buried in Arlington Cemetery. Nelson was a signal officer in France, Germany, and Austria during World War II.

COLES AREA, C. 1969. The Signal Corps established three field laboratories during the 1940s. Field laboratory No. 1, later designated the Camp Coles Signal Laboratory, was located at Newman Springs and Half Mile Roads west of Red Bank. There 46.22 acres of land allowed for observing and measuring pilot balloon ascensions. The land was purchased by the government in June 1942 for $18,400. The area closed in 1975.

POST CHAPEL, 1969. The main post chapel on Malterer Avenue was built in 1962. Protestant, Catholic, Jewish, and Islamic services have been regularly held ever since. Weddings, baptisms, funerals, and special events, including the annual Holocaust remembrance ceremony, are routine occurrences.

SPACE SENTRY MONITORS SATELLITE, 1960. Engineers and technicians of the U.S. Army Signal Corps Research and Development Laboratory watch the signal level as the 60-foot dish-shaped antenna, Space Sentry, picks up signals from the TIROS I weather satellite. The satellite was just coming within radio range of the ground station at Fort Monmouth. From left to right are (seated) William Loehning, George Goubeaud, and Larry Martin; (standing) Charles Krauss, Paul Gorbatch (background), and Arthur Reinbolt.

THE 595TH SIGNAL SUPPORT COMPANY. Members of 595th served as drivers for the fourth Signal Maintenance Symposium held at Fort Monmouth on May 5, 1960. The symposium afforded participants an opportunity to air their difficulties, discuss new approaches to old problems, and find ways of coping with new problems. In addition, concrete results were examined in the area of better practices and in building a new and better concept of maintenance.

FORT MONMOUTH BASEBALL PLAYERS, 1960S. America's favorite pastime has flourished at Fort Monmouth since its earliest days. During World War II, the fort played host to numerous Major League Baseball exhibition games, and famous players spent the war years playing here. On June 6, 1944, as Allied forces invaded Normandy, the Eastern Signal Corps All-Stars played their first major-league opponent, the Boston Braves, at the Charles Wood area of Fort Monmouth.

PROMOTION CEREMONY. Four enlisted personnel of the U.S. Army Communications Systems Agency are promoted to private first class on August 23, 1972. From left to right are Capt. Jane Carter, commander of the Women's Army Corps (WAC) detachment, who was assisting in the promotion of the WACs; Pfc. Betty Jo Vizthum; Pfc. Michael Austin; Pfc. Judy Blankenhorn; and Pfc. Peggy Byrd. Brig. Gen. D. W. Ogden, commanding general of the U.S. Army Communications Systems Agency, officiated.

ELECTRONICS COMMAND EXHIBIT, 1970. Personnel pose with the AN/MPQ-4 radar built by General Electric. It was a dual-beam rapid-scan radar that used vacuum tube technology, an analog computer, mechanical scanning, and unsophisticated extrapolation techniques. Its performance was limited by its need for constant operator alertness, limited multiple-target-handling capability, and degraded performance in rain. The MPQ-4 was used in a limited capacity against hostile artillery in Vietnam.

A DAY AT SUNEAGLES. Pictured are Brig. Gen. Emmett Paige, left, and other unidentified golfers in 1979. Paige was the first African American general in the history of the Signal Corps. He served at Fort Monmouth as commander of the U.S. Army Communications Systems Agency and as the first two-star commander of the Communications Research and Development Command. After leaving Fort Monmouth, he became commander of the Electronics Research and Development Command at Adelphi, Maryland.

CHARITY CAR WASH, MAY 1979. Fort personnel signed up to wash cars for an Army Emergency Relief (AER) campaign fund-raiser. The secretary of war and the U.S. Army chief of staff established AER in 1942. It helps soldiers and their dependants with financial assistance during times of emergency. Assistance is also provided to retired soldiers, widows, dependent children, and spouses.

MAKING ANTENNA ADJUSTMENTS. Electronics command engineer W. P. Czerwinski is making adjustments to a feasibility model of a new beacon antenna on October 14, 1971. The antenna was used for U.S. Army aircraft beacons and with radio beacon set AN/TRN-30. This set may be used in one of two basic configurations—Pathfinder AN/TRN-30 (V)1 or tactical/semifixed AN/TRN-30 (V)2. Primary power was supplied from an external plus-28-volts direct current power source.

SOLDIER SIGHTS A FIREFINDER RADAR. This radar was developed in the 1970s to detect the location of artillery and mortar firing positions. The concept of using a radar system this way originated in the United States at Fort Monmouth in 1944. Approval of the AN/TPQ-36 Mortar Locating Radar Program came in 1971. The U.S. Army selected Hughes Aircraft Company as the developer, following an industry-wide competition in 1972. The name Firefinder replaced the name mortar or artillery locating radar (MALOR).

TESTING EQUIPMENT. A service test is being performed for the air traffic control facility AN/TSQ-97 at Fort Monmouth on March 8, 1973. The AN/TSQ-97 was a four-person portable air traffic control facility used to control air traffic at landing zones in forward areas. Included in the facility were very high frequency/AM/FM and UHF-AM communications capabilities, meteorological equipment, and attendant accessories associated with control of visual flight rule terminal air traffic.

RAWIN SET AN/GMD-1. Staff Sergeant Kinnard, left, on the AN/GMD-1, Sergeant 1st Class Raukin releasing the balloon, and Specialist Mollar, right, releasing the radiosonde, are seen here on July 28, 1970. The AN/GMD-1 was a transportable radio direction finder that automatically tracked a balloon-borne radiosonde transmitter. Meteorological data was then transmitted and received by the AN/GMD-1. These measurements were used to analyze and forecast weather conditions, to guide and plan for aircraft navigation, and to prepare ballistic corrections.

CLASSROOM TRAINING, 1970. Students take Common Basic Electronics Training (COBET) in a classroom designed and built by the training aids division of the U.S. Army Signal Corps School. COBET provided the U.S. Army with a standardized, functional entry-level course for use throughout the Continental Army Command Service School system. The principal objective was to structure a course that could be adapted for basic electronic training for entering any of the 75 different U.S. Army electronic specialist courses.

RADIO NAVIGATION BEACON SET, 1971. The AN/TRN-30(V) shown here was a low-frequency radio navigation beacon set. It transmitted a homing signal used in conjunction with standard airborne direction-finding sets. It provided an amplitude modulated radio frequency signal on any one of 964 channels. The transmission range was 15 to 100 nautical miles. It had a power output of 25 to 180 watts radiated from a 15-, 30-, or 60-foot antenna.

TEEN CLUB. In the early 1960s, chapel No. 4 was turned it into a teen club. The pews were removed, a kitchenette and dining area was built, and a disco ball was hung from the ceiling. The altar became the bandstand. It was later expanded with a coatroom and a room for pool tables. Bruce Springsteen reportedly played there when he was still in high school with a group called the Castiles.

POST COMMISSARY. The post continued to grow with the construction of new facilities through the years. An interdenominational chapel was dedicated in July 1962; a bowling center opened in December 1965; dedication of the post exchange complex took place in February 1970; the commissary opened in April 1971; Green Acres, the command office building, officially opened in November 1973; and the credit union building and the post library opened in June 1974.

Five

COMMANDERS TO POST LANDMARKS

CHANGE OF COMMAND CEREMONY, 1982. Pictured are, from left to right, Maj. Gen. Donald Babers, Gen. Donald R. Keith (Army Materiel Command commanding general), and Maj. Gen. Lawrence Skibbie. Skibbie was the 30th commanding officer of Fort Monmouth and the second commanding general of the Communications-Electronics Command (CECOM). He served in this position from October 1982 to June 1984. Babers was the first commanding general of CECOM when it was established in 1981.

THE GENERAL'S STAFF. Maj. Gen. Lawrence Skibbie (first row, fifth from right) and the combined CECOM staff pose for a photograph on June 23, 1983. Before coming to Fort Monmouth, he served in the office of the deputy chief of staff for research, development, and acquisition in Washington, D.C., from 1978 to 1982. After his tour of duty at Fort Monmouth, Skibbie was promoted to lieutenant general and assigned as the deputy commanding general for readiness of the Army Materiel Command.

MORGAN AND THOMAS CHANGE OF COMMAND. Maj. Gen. Robert D. Morgan (right) became the 31st commanding officer of Fort Monmouth and the third commanding general of CECOM. Morgan was the first commanding officer at Fort Monmouth to have been a U.S. Army aviator. Maj. Gen. Billy M. Thomas assumed command in May 1987. He was promoted to lieutenant general in 1990 and assigned as the deputy commanding general for research, development, and acquisition of the Army Materiel Command in Alexandria, Virginia.

UNIDENTIFIED SOLDIER WITH GUARDRAIL V TACTICAL COMMANDERS TERMINAL. Guardrail is an airborne intelligence collection system that provides support to early entry forces, forward deployed forces, and military intelligence. Guardrail is called a common sensor because it can intercept both classes of signal, including communications intelligence, low-frequency radio transmissions, and cell phone calls, as well as electronics intelligence and radar transmissions. It was fielded to Korea in 1988.

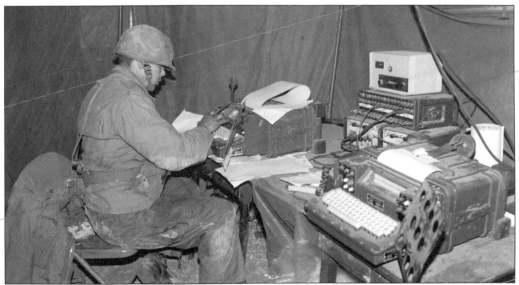

POSITION LOCATION REPORTING SYSTEM. Pictured is an unidentified soldier with the 9th Infantry Division at Yakima Firing Center in Washington for the integration of Position Location Reporting System (PLRS) in May 1982. The office of the project manager for PLRS was one of eight of Fort Monmouth's project managers. It was responsible for monitoring the overall development, production, and fielding of PLRS, a joint U.S. Army/Marine Corps program. PLRS was required to enhance the command, control, and communications function and improve force effectiveness in difficult combat environments such as night operations.

JOHNSTON GATE REDEDICATION. The new Johnston Gate was built in 1985 and rededicated to Col. Gordon Johnston in a formal ceremony in 1986. From left to right are Richard F. Cottrell, Monmouth County undersheriff; Dave Drake, Wallace and Watson Associates; Maj. Gen. Robert D. Morgan; Steven Weeks of H. V. Weeks; Dorothy Blair Manson, mayor of Shrewsbury; S. Thomas Gagliano, New Jersey state senator; Rose Morgan; and Angleos M. Gregos of the Sharp Construction Company.

BARKER CIRCLE, 1985. These barracks buildings were constructed in 1927 and represent the first permanent buildings constructed at Fort Monmouth. They are three stories tall with a full three-story porch supported by concrete piers that span the main facade. The group of buildings was named in 1942 in honor of U.S. Military Academy cadet Ernest S. Barker, who was killed in a training accident. In 1958, the original slate roofs were replaced with asphalt-shingled ones.

KAPLAN HALL, 1985. Once the site of the post theater, Kaplan Hall has, since 1982, housed the U.S. Army Communications-Electronics Museum. It was constructed in 1933 with funds from the Army Motion Picture Service. The building was named for Maj. Benjamin Kaplan (1902–1952) on December 21, 1953, by General Orders No. 221. As post engineer, Kaplan oversaw construction of what is now known as the historic district of Fort Monmouth.

NEW MUSEUM EXHIBITS, 1989. Personnel review new exterior exhibits at the museum. Speakers at the dedication ceremony included Brig. Gen. Melvin Leon Byrd, deputy commanding general of CECOM, and Brig. Gen. William H. Campbell, program executive officer of intelligence and electronic warfare at Vint Hill Farms station in Warrenton, Virginia. Exterior exhibits included the radar set AN/TPQ-37, Vulcan Air Defense System, TACJAM countermeasure set AN/MLQ-34 advanced development model, and satellite dish AN/TSC-54.

AERIAL OF 1200 AREA, 1984. The 1200 area features the barracks and classroom buildings originally constructed for the Signal School in 1953. Backfill following the departure of the Signal School included the military academy preparatory school (1975), the chaplain center and school (1979–1996), the 513th Military Intelligence Brigade (1982–1993), and the Federal Bureau of Investigation's regional computer support center. The location was rehabilitated in 1996 to house elements of CECOM.

AERIAL OF VAIL HALL, 1985. Vail Hall is home to the directorate of information management. The building was constructed in 1952, and per General Orders No. 19, dated June 21, 1956, it memorializes Alfred Vail (1807–1859). Vail was the distinguished New Jersey inventor whose great mechanical and financial contributions to wire communications substantially accelerated the first experiments in telegraphy.

AERIAL OF SQUIER HALL, 1985. Located on Sherrill Drive, Squier Hall was built in 1935 to house the Signal Corps Engineering Laboratories. It is now home to the Program Executive Offices (PEO) for Enterprise Information Systems and the Defense Information Systems Agency. It was named in honor of Maj. Gen. George Owen Squier, chief signal officer from 1917 to 1923. New York architects Rodgers and Poor designed the building.

HUSKY BROOK POND, 1985. Husky Brook Pond is located near the Nicodemus Gate. It underwent a massive cleanup from 1966 through the early 1970s that sought to convert a 10-acre wasteland into a handsome, useful recreation area. Today the area boasts several picnic sites and tranquil views.

AERIAL OF COMMANDING OFFICER'S HOME, 1987. Building 230 was constructed for the commanding officer in 1936 at the western end of Voris Park. This Georgian Revival–style building is seven bays wide and has a one-story garage wing. A pedimented gable roof with a lunette and a porch with double columns topped by a balustrade mark the entrance. The building also features paired end chimneys and a dentil cornice. Parker Creek can be seen in the background.

OFFICERS' HOUSING, 1985. Housing for officers was constructed between 1929 and 1932 as four-family apartment buildings for student officers. The buildings are laid out in two rows with a service lane between the rows to provide access to garages. The buildings, located north of Greely Field, are two stories with paired central entrances. Each pair of entry doors shares a covered stoop that features simple trim and Georgian Colonial Revival detailing.

PATTERSON ARMY COMMUNITY HOSPITAL, 1985. Patterson Army Community Hospital was built in 1958 and continues today as Patterson Army Health Clinic. The clinic provides ambulatory and preventive health care services to approximately 10,000 eligible beneficiaries and sees approximately 120 patients per working day. The facility was named in honor of Maj. Gen. Robert Urie Patterson, U.S. Army Medical Corps (1877–1950). Patterson received two Silver Stars for conspicuous gallantry in action in the Philippines.

RUSSEL HALL, 1985. Russel Hall was originally the post headquarters building. Philadelphia architect Harry Sternfield designed the building, which was completed in 1936 in collaboration with the office of the constructing quartermaster. Sculptured reliefs located on the exterior depict the Signal Corps in the Civil War and World War I. Today Russel Hall is the Fort Monmouth Garrison Headquarters. Russel Hall memorializes Maj. Gen. Edgar Russel, chief signal officer of the AEF during World War I.

CHARLES WOOD CHAPEL. This chapel, adjacent to the Albert J. Myer Center, was built in 1942 to accommodate the massive influx of troops to that area of post. It is of the standard 700-series Quartermaster Corps design. The stained glass in the chapel came from Fort Holabird in 1974. The chapel was decommissioned on May 18, 2008.

ALBERT J. MYER CENTER, 1989. The Charles Wood area's Albert J. Myer Center, also known as the hexagon or building 2700, was constructed in 1954 for the Signal Corps Laboratories. Today it is the headquarters of the Communications-Electronics Research, Development, and Engineering Center (CERDEC) and the PEO for Command, Control and Communications Tactical and Intelligence, Electronic Warfare and Sensors. It was dedicated in 1988 in honor of the founder of the Signal Corps, Brig Gen. Albert J. Myer.

Six

GULF WAR TO POST CEREMONIES

WELCOME HOME DESERT STORM WARRIORS. Over 1,000 people turned out to greet the troops returning from a yearlong deployment to the Persian Gulf on March 9, 1991. New Jersey governor James Florio and Sen. Frank Lautenberg were on-site to welcome each soldier home. A military police escort transported the troops and their families from McGuire Air Force Base back to Fort Monmouth, where they were greeted by a cheering crowd and 200 fire trucks.

WAITING AT THE JOHNSTON GATE. The Fort Monmouth community awaits the return of Desert Storm troopers from Saudi Arabia in March 1991. The command's employees had worked tirelessly to equip soldiers with everything from radios and jammers to night vision and intelligence systems. On the eve of the ground war, CECOM had 59 military, 103 civilian, and 122 contractor personnel in or on their way to the Kuwaiti theater of operations.

COMMUNITY OUTREACH PROGRAM. Sgt. Ann Resko, 513th Military Intelligence Brigade, models some of the equipment and clothing soldiers used in Saudi Arabia at the Jonas Salk Middle School in Old Bridge in October 1990. In the lead-up to war, several of the local elementary and middle schools in Monmouth County signed up to write letters, collect supplies, and create care packages for the troops being sent to Saudi Arabia.

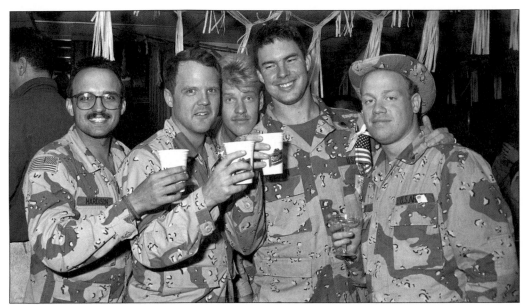

DESERT STORM TROOPERS ARRIVE HOME. Members of the 513th Military Intelligence Brigade celebrate at their welcome-home party on March 26, 1991. The brigade fulfilled its wartime mission and provided full-spectrum intelligence support to U.S. Army Central Command, winning three Southwest Asian Service battle streamers. The 513th was activated at Fort Monmouth in September 1982, resulting in an additional 375 military personnel at the post. The brigade was realigned to Fort Gordon, Georgia, in 1994.

DEVELOPING EQUIPMENT FOR OPERATION DESERT STORM. Three staff members of the Center for Command, Control and Communications Systems pitch in to assemble new communications equipment needed in Saudi Arabia. From left to right, they are William Guthrie, CECOM contractor; Palemon Dubowicz, electronics technician; and Joseph Lee, designer of the equipment. The 11th Transportation Battalion requested that CECOM design and build the systems for its lighter air-cushioned vehicles 30.

HELLO SAUDI ARABIA. Personnel from the office of the provost marshal gathered to send greetings to colleagues in Saudi Arabia on November 5, 1990. By the end of operations, the command had processed close to 180,000 requisitions, shipped 6 million pieces of equipment (including 4 million batteries), and procured a total of 10.8 million pieces of equipment worth $326 million. A communications security management office had also been established in theater on November 15, 1990.

MILITARY AFFILIATE RADIO SYSTEM STATION. The Military Affiliate Radio System (MARS) station at Fort Monmouth, K2USA, operated around the clock with 51 volunteers during Operation Desert Storm. Volunteers included Fort Monmouth's commander Maj. Gen. (later Lt. Gen.) Alfred J. Mallette, shown here. Operators relayed messages between servicemen abroad and their loved ones at home and provided a worldwide radio communications capability in times of emergency. The predecessor to MARS started at Fort Monmouth in 1925.

GOV. CHRISTINE TODD WHITMAN VISIT. From left to right are Col. Jack Demsey, Victor Ferlise, Maj. Gen. Robert Nabors, Gov. Christine Todd Whitman, and Frank Fiorilli in front of Mallette Hall on June 22, 1999. The governor was provided a command overview briefing that discussed critical technologies, base realignment and closure (BRAC), and new construction on post. She then toured 17 indoor and outdoor exhibits highlighting the command's efforts to introduce new technologies.

PERSONNEL GATHERED AT THE AMPHITHEATER. This audience was gathered for the presentation of the command's President's Quality Award. The Logistics and Readiness Center (LRC) competed for and won the President's Quality Improvement Prototype Award for 1996. Maj. Gen. Gerard P. Brohm received the award on June 5, 1996, during the ninth annual Conference on Federal Quality. Brohm said the award "recognizes the superb management and work force as well as the technical excellence and outstanding customer service of our LRC organization."

ANECHOIC CHAMBER. Maj. Gen. Robert L. Van Antwerp, director of the office of competitive sourcing, office of the assistant secretary of the U.S. Army (research, development, and acquisition), visited the anechoic chamber at the Intelligence and Information Warfare Directorate on October 5, 1999. This 3,000-square-foot facility is the largest in the state of New Jersey and is used to conduct sensitive radio frequency, electromagnetic compatibility, and interference measurement for federal government agencies, industry, and academia.

SOLDIERS FIRING CEREMONIAL HOWITZERS. Howitzers were fired in honor of the change of command ceremony between Maj. Gen. Billy M. Thomas and Maj. Gen. Alfred J. Mallette on July 10, 1990. Thomas assumed command of CECOM and Fort Monmouth in May 1987. He was promoted to lieutenant general on July 10, 1990, and assumed duties as the deputy commanding general for research, development, and acquisition of the Army Materiel Command in Alexandria, Virginia.

OBSERVING THE LAND WARRIOR SYSTEM, 1999. Victor Ferlise (second from right), deputy to the commanding general, and other Fort Monmouth personnel observe a soldier wearing the Land Warrior system during the Military Communications Conference (MILCOM) in Atlantic City. The team at Fort Monmouth hosts MILCOM every fifth year. The event provides an opportunity for both the Department of Defense and its industry and academic partners to share information about command, control, communications, computers, intelligence, surveillance, and reconnaissance (C4ISR) systems. Over 3,000 attendees participate at each conference.

VETERANS DAY SERVICE, GREELY FIELD, 1992. Cadet candidates fire their M-16 rifles during the Veterans Day ceremony held on November 11. Veterans Day was originally designated as Armistice Day to commemorate the end of World War I. The Germans signed the armistice on the 11th hour of the 11th day of the 11th month in 1918. It was redesignated Veterans Day in 1954 to honor veterans of all wars.

GREELY FIELD, 389TH ARMY BAND, 1990. The 389th Army Band traces its history to its 1901 organization at Fort Meade, Maryland, as the 13th Cavalry Band. The 389th came to Fort Monmouth in August 1930 as the Signal Corps Band. It was designated the 389th Army Band in 1944. It is now the official band of the Army Materiel Command. The band moved to Aberdeen Proving Ground in Maryland in October 1994 as part of a nationwide realignment of U.S. Army bands.

MEMORIAL DAY SERVICES, 1992. This service was held in front of the World War II memorial, located at the northern border of Greely Field. The memorial honors those members of the Signal Corps who gave their lives during World War II. It was dedicated at the celebration of the 35th anniversary of Fort Monmouth in 1952. Relatives and friends of the honored dead and members of Fort Monmouth and other Signal Corps installations contributed to building the monument.

FORT MONMOUTH FIREFIGHTERS, 1991. Fire inspector Jack Snow, left, and fire inspector Thomas Braumuller conduct a fire safety program at the child development center. The mission of Fort Monmouth's fire and emergency services is to provide a safe working and living environment for the Fort Monmouth community, to establish a fire prevention and safety education program, and to respond to any emergency rapidly to preserve life and property.

THE FORT MONMOUTH OFFICERS' WIVES CLUB. Members of the Fort Monmouth Officers' Wives Club (FMOWC) hold a quilt raffle at Gibbs Hall on March 20, 1996. The FMOWC has a long history of supporting the Fort Monmouth community through charitable fund-raisers, educational, social, and cultural events, and sponsoring fort children. Today the FMOWC Welfare Fund sponsors scholarships for military dependent spouses and high school seniors. Wives and spouses clubs provide friendship, service, and support to their members and the local community.

CHAPLAIN SCHOOL CLASS, 1993. The U.S. Army Chaplain Center and School, the U.S. Army's only training center for the clergy, moved to Fort Monmouth in 1979 from Fort Wadsworth, New York. It conducted resident training for over 1,000 students per year, including 700 enlisted chaplain activity specialists and 300 chaplains in both the officer basic and advanced courses. The school, which transferred to Fort Jackson, South Carolina, during the 1990s, was headquartered in what was then designated as Watters Hall (building 1207).

VETERANS DAY SERVICES, 1992. Veterans listen to a service taking place on Greely Field. Located between Sherrill and Saltzman Avenues, Greely Field honors Maj. Gen. Adolphus W. Greely, chief signal officer from 1887 to 1906. The field was dedicated on April 6, 1949. As a lieutenant, Greely led the 1881–1884 Signal Corps Meteorological Expedition to the Arctic. He received the Congressional Medal of Honor on his 91st birthday, March 27, 1935.

POST MARINA, 1997. The marina building was constructed in 1986. The Fort Monmouth Department of Public Works used money from the Central Post Fund to buy the marina from the Civilian Welfare Fund in the 1960s. Today it provides storage and dockage for private boats up to 35 feet and rental boats for pleasure or fishing on the Shrewsbury and Navesink Rivers. Various watercraft can be rented for recreational use.

DEDICATION OF MALLETTE HALL. Personnel gather for the dedication of Mallette Hall (building 1207) on October 17, 1996. The building honors Lt. Gen. Alfred J. Mallette, commander of CECOM from July 10, 1990, to July 22, 1992. The building currently serves as the headquarters of the U.S. Army CECOM Life Cycle Management Command. It is located in the 1200 area along the north side of the Avenue of Memories.

SOLDIERS PARK, 1991. Soldiers Park is located at the intersection of the Avenue of Memories and Wilson Avenue, opposite the bowling center. It honors "the Fort Monmouth soldiers and civilians who deployed and fought worldwide and the families who kept the home fires burning bright." Adjacent to Soldiers Park is a small monument dedicated to Wesley L. Kain, killed in action on December 16, 1944.

GOLFERS IN FRONT OF GIBBS HALL, 1995. Gibbs Hall (the Fort Monmouth Officers' Club) began as a private country club known as Suneagles, built by Max Phillips in the 1920s. The country club consisted of a clubhouse (which is still largely intact as part of Gibbs Hall), an 18-hole golf course, a polo field, and an airfield. The U.S. Army acquired the site in 1941. Gibbs Hall memorializes Maj. Gen. George S. Gibbs, chief signal officer from 1928 to 1931.

LANE HALL, 1995. Lane Hall functions as the community activity center. The building was dedicated in 1983 after the old enlisted mess hall that had originally memorialized Pvt. 2nd Class Morgan D. Lane was razed. Lane was the first member of the Signal Corps to receive the Medal of Honor. He fought with the Union army during the Civil War and was rewarded for capturing the Confederate flag from the gunboat *Nansemond* near Jetersville, Virginia.

FLAG AT HALF-MAST. These howitzers were positioned in preparation for a 21-gun salute at Russel Hall in April 1994 in honor of the passing of Pres. Richard Nixon. The guns are placed in front of Cowan Park. Dedicated on June 24, 1961, Cowan Park memorializes Col. Arthur S. Cowan, who commanded the Signal Corps camp at Little Silver from September 16, 1917, to June 28, 1918, and from September 2, 1929, to April 30, 1937.

ALLISON HALL, 1992. Allison Hall once housed the first permanent hospital building, the U.S. Army Management Agency, and the Satellite Communications Agency. It is currently home to the program manager for Defense Communications and Army Transmission Systems. Built in 1928 with a major addition in 1934, it is located at the intersection of Barton and Allen Avenues. General orders in 1961 dedicated the building to Maj. Gen. James B. Allison, Fort Monmouth commander from 1925 to 1926 and chief signal officer from 1935 to 1937.

CHARLES WOOD HOUSING, 1992. The Charles Wood area consists of 512 acres acquired by the U.S. Army in 1941 to accommodate wartime expansion. Personnel constructed a cantonment area for 7,000 troops within 90 days of the purchase. The U.S. Army dedicated the area to the memory of Lt. Col. Charles W. Wood, an assistant executive officer at Fort Monmouth. Wood died suddenly on June 1, 1942, while on temporary duty in Washington, D.C.

Seven

CADET CANDIDATE TRAINING TO SOUTHWEST ASIA

JOHNSTON GATE SANDBAGGED AFTER 9/11. Shortly after the September 11, 2001, attacks, the provost marshal, CECOM force protection staff, and garrison made the joint decision to close the fort. This decision reversed 40 years of an open-post tradition. The command's emergency operations center sprang into operation 24 hours a day, seven days a week. Technologies developed at Fort Monmouth were used at the World Trade Center to aid in recovery efforts.

GEN. ERIC SHINSEKI, ARMY CHIEF OF STAFF. Maj. Gen. Robert Nabors, left, greets Gen. Eric Shinseki during his visit to the command in July 2000. Shinseki toured the CECOM Research, Development, and Engineering Center where the Universal Soldier systems/uncooled camera was showcased. Shinseki's visit also included a stop at the command's C4ISR On-the-Move demonstration at Fort Dix.

MAJ. GEN. WILLIAM H. RUSS RETIREMENT CEREMONY. Maj. Gen. William H. Russ assumed command of CECOM in July 2001 and saw the command through the harrowing days after 9/11 and the initial years of Operations Enduring and Iraqi Freedom. After the attacks, Russ immediately convened his senior leaders to assess how the command could assist the recovery efforts.

29-30 MAY 2002

RETIRED GENERAL OFFICER/SENIOR EXECUTIVE SERVICE CONFERENCE. Russ poses in front of Gibbs Hall with retired general officers and members of the Senior Executive Service in May 2002. The theme of the conference was "Team C4IEWS—Enabling the Transformation . . . The Road to Network Centric Warfare." The purpose of these conferences is to discuss issues impacting the C4ISR community and to tap the expertise of retired personnel to resolve challenges.

MAJ. GEN. MICHAEL R. MAZZUCCHI PROMOTION CEREMONY. Maj. Gen. Michael R. Mazzucchi assumed command in June 2004 and became the first commander to wear both the hat of the C-E Life Cycle Management Command and the hat of the program executive officer for Command, Control and Communications Tactical. The U.S. Army established life-cycle management commands to overcome the culture of acquisition versus logistics. The payoff would be getting products to the soldier faster and streamlining the acquisition and logistics process.

BRAVO COMPANY, 181ST LIGHT INFANTRY REGIMENT. The mobilization of reserves for homeland defense occurred in response to the September 11 terrorist attacks. Dubbed Operation Noble Eagle, it began in October 2001 for Fort Monmouth with the arrival of Bravo Company, 1st Battalion, 181st Light Infantry Regiment from Boston. The company's mission was to protect the Fort Monmouth community, its facilities, and personnel stationed on post.

JON BON JOVI PERFORMANCE. The rock band Bon Jovi entertained a full house at the Expo Theater in October 2005. Band members Jon Bon Jovi, Richie Sambora, Tico Torres, and David Bryan also met with Maj Gen. Michael R. Mazzucchi and garrison officials and visited with cadet candidates from the United States Military Academy Preparatory School (USMAPS).

THE 854TH ENGINEERING BATTALION. Members of the 854th Engineering Battalion, Combat, Heavy, Army Reserve unit based in Kingston, New York, pose with Col. Renita Foster of the public affairs office in 2002. This reserve battalion, made up of electricians, plumbers, and carpenters, worked on various engineering construction projects while training at Fort Monmouth. Its 18-hour workdays included building, plumbing, electrical work, carpentry, masonry, widening roads, renovating and bulldozing buildings, and horizontal construction.

INTERN GREENING COURSE, 2005. Interns listen to a pigeon expert at the U.S. Army Communications-Electronics Museum in 2005. Part of CERDEC's greening course included learning about how soldiers communicated before the age of satellite telephones and FM radios. The course was established in 2004 by Dwayne A. Davis, former lead outreach program coordinator. The course familiarizes civilian personnel with the activities of soldiers.

INTERN HELICOPTER RIDE. Part of the greening course includes a ride in a Huey helicopter over the New Jersey coast. The course was so well received by interns that it became mandatory for all new hires. In addition to making personnel more efficient at providing equipment to meet the soldiers' mission, the greening course and other related programs also lets soldiers know that their equipment is being built by someone who genuinely understands their needs.

TOP OFF EXERCISE, 2005. From left to right, Fort Monmouth firefighters Paul Wind, Dave Bahrenburg, William Chyzik, Michael Marra, Jason Brown, and William Donahue pose during the Top Off exercise. Top Off is an annual exercise sponsored by the Department of Homeland Security. The exercise tests the preparedness and interoperability of various emergency response and law enforcement activities during a live, multifaceted mock incident.

BATTLE OF THE BULGE MONUMENT, 2002. Col. Ricki Sullivan (in uniform, left) and Col. James Costigan (in uniform, right) gather with Battle of the Bulge veterans and spouses in honor of the 58th anniversary of the battle. This monument honors the men and women of the United States armed forces who participated in the Battle of the Bulge from December 16, 1944, to January 25, 1945. The monument was dedicated on May 6, 2001.

FAMILY VISITS MEMORIAL ON AVENUE OF MEMORIES. The Avenue of Memories was designated by general order in 1949 in honor of the officers and men of the Signal Corps who gave their lives during World War II in the service of their country. The U.S. Army dedicated the avenue on April 6, 1949, when the first marker was placed in memory of Maj. Edmund P. Karr. It was originally designated as Memorial Drive.

HURRICANE KATRINA RELIEF EFFORTS. Personnel set up satellite communications equipment in support of relief efforts following Hurricane Katrina. The command responded immediately with C4ISR systems and support following the storm. This included providing generators and communications systems. When the storm disrupted the Defense Information System Agency hub in New Orleans, software engineers provided vital support to reestablish the connectivity of systems through which requisitions for Southwest Asia were processed.

NEW INTERN CLASS, 2002. Edward Elgart, director of the acquisition center, addresses new acquisition center interns at conference room A in Mallette Hall. The command hired 82 interns in fiscal year 2002. An annual professional development day is held for interns at Gibbs Hall. The theme for the day in 2002 was "Interns Empowering the Future." The various topics discussed included U.S. Army transformation, empowerment, mentoring, and career advice. Over 200 personnel attended.

WAR MEMORIAL. This large memorial on the grounds of USMAPS is located off Abbey Road. Dedicated in June 1994, the memorial lists the names of those graduates lost during World War II, the Korean War, the Vietnam War, and current operations in Southwest Asia.

USMAPS HEADQUARTERS. Cadet candidates from USMAPS pose in front of their headquarters in 2005. USMAPS, established in 1945, moved to Fort Monmouth from Fort Belvoir, Virginia, in 1975. Here selected enlisted members of the U.S. Army spend a year preparing physically, academically, and militarily to enter the United States Military Academy at West Point, New York.

USMAPS RECEPTION DAY. Cadet candidates are reading the *Cadet Candidate Handbook* on Reception Day (R-Day) in 2005. Beginning on R-Day, cadet candidates learn the basics of drilling and saluting and the U.S. Army rank system. At the post exchange, they receive everything from work uniforms and boots to canteens and toiletries. Following four weeks of cadet candidate basic training (CCBT), the candidates take a three-hour exam on military terms, protocol, and tactics. They then begin academic classes.

ROPE CLIMBING. Part of CCBT is an eight-day field training exercise at Fort Dix. Here cadet candidates learn military skills, leadership, and teamwork. They participate in timed events that include an obstacle course of mazes, rope climbing, cargo nets, balancing logs, vaulting ropes, walls, and horizontal ladders. They also learn land navigation, how to fire the M-16 rifle, pugilism, hand-to-hand combat, and water survival.

PREPARING MEALS READY TO EAT. Cadet candidates learn how to prepare meals ready to eat (MRE) during CCBT in 2005. The U.S. Army debuted MRE in 1981 for use in combat. They replaced earlier types of rations like the meal combat individual rations and C rations. Today MRE come in 24 different entrée options. A flameless ration heater comes with the package to heat the food. Early experiments with unpopular entrée options caused soldiers to nickname them "meals rejected by the enemy."

USMAPS GRADUATION PARADE. During graduation week in 2005, cadet candidates participated in a graduation review at Greely Field, an awards ceremony, a graduation dinner and dance, and the formal graduation ceremony and reception. The award ceremony recognizes cadet candidates for military and academic leadership and overall excellence. One cadet candidate is selected by his or her peers for making the greatest contribution to the class. Other awards include first in English and math and most improved student.

Closing the New York Stock Exchange. The CECOM Life Cycle Management Command and Fort Monmouth soldiers are at the New York Stock Exchange (NYSE) closing bell ceremony on the U.S. Army's birthday, June 14, 2007. From left to right are Maj. Curtiss Bailey, Lt. Col. Gregory Mathers, Lt. Col. Rodney Mentzer, Command Sgt. Maj. Ray D. Lane, Maj. Gen. Michael R. Mazzucchi, Col. William Hoppe, Lt. Col. Michelle Nassar, Capt. Virginia MacNeil, and Maj. Brent Skinner, accompanied by president and co-chief operating officer of NYSE Euronext Catherine R. Kinney.

Senior Leader Off-Site. The CECOM Life Cycle Management Command and C4ISR senior leadership pose for a picture during the Senior Leader Forum held at Picatinny Arsenal, New Jersey, on October 25–27, 2007. The forum allowed senior leaders to discuss a number of important topics affecting the command, including leading change and the many facets of BRAC. The guest speaker was Maj. Gen. Robert Nabors (Ret.), former commanding general of CECOM.

AVENUE OF MEMORIES. The organizations located along the Avenue of Memories are primarily directorates of the Logistics and Readiness Center. These activities fulfill the sustainment portion of the command's life-cycle mission. This includes filling requisitions for equipment from units located worldwide, writing and editing manuals for those systems, filling foreign military sales requests, new equipment training, forward maintenance, supply and logistics support, provisioning, production planning and acceptance, manufacturing base support, configuration management, product quality management, and more.

McAFEE CENTER. The McAfee Center (building 600) houses the Intelligence and Information Warfare Directorate of CERDEC. It is located on Sherrill Avenue. Dedicated on July 28, 1997, the center honors renowned physicist Dr. Walter McAfee. McAfee held numerous supervisory positions during his 42 years at Fort Monmouth and made the mathematical calculations that resulted in the first contact with the moon.

Welcome-Home Sign, 2004. This sign hung at the entrance to the 754th Explosive Ordnance Disposal Company building to welcome the soldiers home from their second deployment to Afghanistan. The 754th arrived at Fort Monmouth from Camp Kilmer in 1966 and relocated to Fort Drum, New York, in 2008. Its mission is explosive ordnance disposal and bomb threat search techniques. The unit has deployed to Southwest Asia several times since the September 11, 2001, terrorist attacks.

Repairing Night Vision Goggles. Technicians repaired thousands of night vision goggles during a five-week assignment to Fort Lewis, Washington, in 2008. Soldiers returning from deployment turned to 11 technicians supporting the Communications Electronics Evaluation Repair Team to repair 2,546 monocular-style AN/PVS-14 goggles belonging to the 4th Brigade, 2nd Infantry Division (Stryker). The team worked 12-hour days, repairing components such as gaskets and defective optical instruments, testing image intensifier tubes, and replacing battery housings.

SOLDIER USING BLUE FORCE TRACKING SYSTEM. These situational awareness systems provide a visual representation of friendly and enemy forces on computer screens inside vehicles and command posts and on hand-held versions. Supported by the entire Fort Monmouth team, these systems give commanders unprecedented situational awareness on the battlefield and allow them to synchronize their forces. The use of these systems resulted in the virtual elimination of friendly fire incidents during Operation Iraqi Freedom.

CECOM LOGISTICS ASSISTANCE REPRESENTATIVE, 2009. Power and environmental logistics assistance representative (LAR) Gary Dygert sets up an American Forces Network satellite dish at Forward Operating Base Shank, Afghanistan. This dish would provide entertainment and internal information for the third of the 10th Mountain Division at Fort Drum, New York. In addition to providing on-site assistance with the maintenance and sustainment of U.S. Army generators, heating, and air-conditioning units, Dygert also supported this unit with the setup of its electric grid.

STRATEGIC PLANNING DISCUSSION, 2007. Then brigadier general Nick Justice of PEO Command, Control and Communications Tactical, center, participates in a strategic planning discussion following a daily battle update briefing at the U.S. Army National Training Center in Fort Irwin, California. Justice was promoted to major general in June 2007. He leads an organization of more than 2,300 employees that fields an extensive range of battle command and communications capabilities with an annual budget exceeding $6 billion.

CECOM PERSONNEL, KUWAIT, OCTOBER 2007. Michael Anthony (left), senior command representative–Southwest Asia, and Col. Robert Rhodes, deputy director of the Logistics and Readiness Center, stand in front of the command's Electronic Sustainment Support Center (ESSC). The ESSC is a multiuse facility located at Camp Arifjan, Kuwait. It serves as the hub for CECOM's broad mission in theater. Other colocated organizations include the CECOM Regional Support Center, Generator Repair Facility, and the reset team.

SENIOR LEADERS WITH TOBYHANNA TEAM. The CECOM Life Cycle Management Command commander visits the Tobyhanna Army Depot Forward Repair Activity (FRA) at Camp Arifjan, Kuwait, in the fall of 2007. This facility is the largest repair activity in Southwest Asia and is colocated with the command's ESSC. From left to right are (first row) Bryan Califano, Donald Cirba, Maj. Gen. Dennis L. Via, Command Sgt. Maj. Ray D. Lane, and Jay Reviello; (second row) Col. Melvin Leary, Clint Russell, Patricia Craig, Mark Hazen, and James Bzdick.

GEN. GEORGE W. CASEY JR. VISITS FORT. S.Sgt. John Jenkins explains technology supported by the fort community to U.S. Army chief of staff Gen. George W. Casey Jr. during his visit in November 2008. Casey spoke with Fort Monmouth leaders, its workforce, and future officers at Pruden Auditorium about the U.S. Army's four imperatives: sustain, prepare, reset, and transform. Maj. Gen. Dennis L. Via provided Casey with a command overview and a BRAC implementation overview during his visit.

ACROSS AMERICA, PEOPLE ARE DISCOVERING SOMETHING WONDERFUL. THEIR HERITAGE.

Arcadia Publishing is the leading local history publisher in the United States. With more than 3,000 titles in print and hundreds of new titles released every year, Arcadia has extensive specialized experience chronicling the history of communities and celebrating America's hidden stories, bringing to life the people, places, and events from the past. To discover the history of other communities across the nation, please visit:

www.arcadiapublishing.com

Customized search tools allow you to find regional history books about the town where you grew up, the cities where your friends and family live, the town where your parents met, or even that retirement spot you've been dreaming about.